JOHN ANDREWS

Architecture a performing art

Oxford University Press
New York

Jennifer Taylor & John Andrews

Oxford University Press
Oxford London Glasgow New York Toronto Delhi Bombay
Calcutta Madras Karachi Kuala Lumpur Singapore
Hong Kong Tokyo Nairobi Dar es Salaam Cape Town
Melbourne Auckland
and associate companies in
Beirut Berlin Ibadan Mexico City

Library of Congress
Cataloguing in Publication data

Taylor, Jennifer
    John Andrews architecture
    a performing art.

    1. Taylor, Jennifer I. Andrews, John,
    joint author. II. Title.
    NA 1605.A5A4 1979
    720′.92′4 78-13466
    ISBN 0 19 550557 3

Designed by Harry Williamson
Edited by Annette Robinson
Produced by John Ferguson Pty Ltd
133 Macquarie Street, Sydney, New South Wales
Typeset by B&D Modgraphic Pty Ltd, Adelaide, South Australia
Published by Oxford University Press, Inc.
200 Madison Avenue, N.Y. 10016
Printed in Hong Kong

Most of the photographs in this book are by David
Moore. The authors thank him, and also Peter
Courtney, Steve Rosenthal, John Reeves and Geoff
Willing.

The text in this book has been set in two distinct
typefaces to distinguish the general text (large face),
written by Jennifer Taylor, from the project
descriptions (small face), dictated by John Andrews
and edited by Jennifer Taylor.

720.92
A567

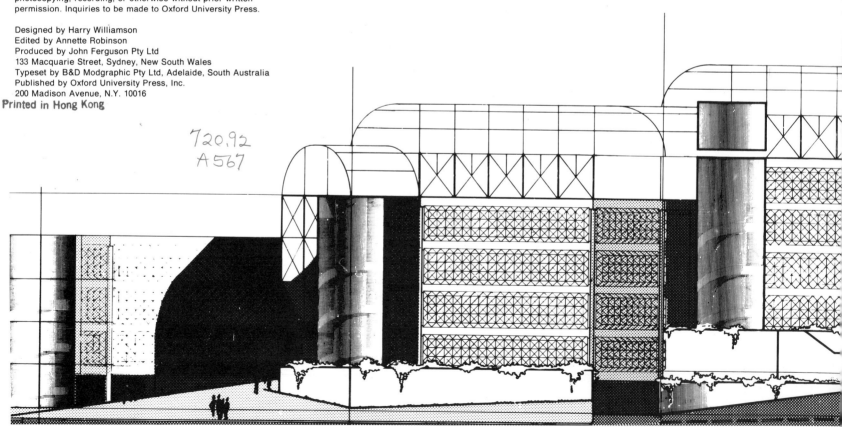

Contents

4 Preface

6 Introduction

14 John Andrews, architect

20 Training and early projects

North America

28 Breakthrough
Scarborough College

48 Kids and community
Bellmere Primary School

54 Shaping up for social concerns
Guelph University student residence

70 Then everything happened
African Place Expo '67

77 Precedent for passengers
Miami Port Passenger Terminal

84 Circulation is . . .
Metro Centre

92 Building a belief
Gund Hall, Harvard

108 And so to . . .

Australia

110 The new context

111 Building in context
King George Tower

123 Campuses and colleges
*Australian National University
student residence*
*Canberra College of Advanced Education
student residence*

133 Then everything happened again

137 More than a building
Cameron Offices

154 Low energy let down

157 Forming up and filling in
*Royal Melbourne Institute of Technology
Library and Student Union*

163 Culture and climate

169 International outer space

173 And on to . . .

174 Projects, publications, film

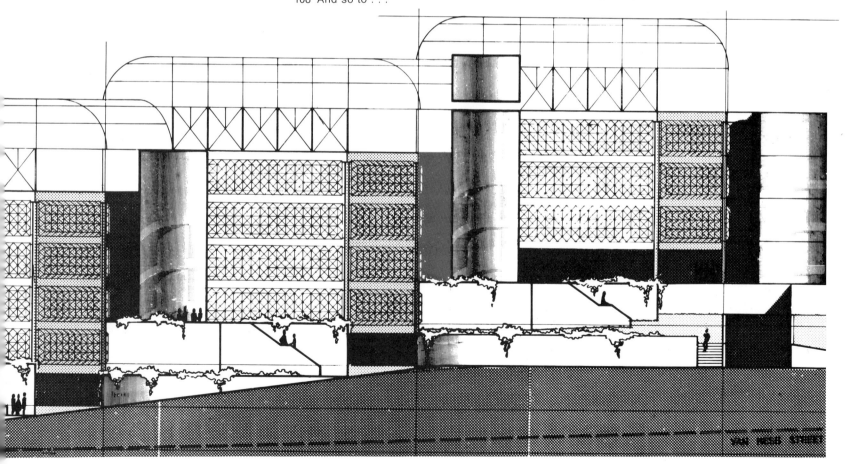

Preface

My years as President of the University of Toronto coincided roughly with the great expansion of the sixties, and I spent a high proportion of my time dealing with builders, planners, and architects. It was not a happy experience. The governing body of the University was responsible for financial matters, and, hence, for all construction, and they insisted that architects and planners should, after an initial period, work apart from the 'user's committees', as we called the group of academics for whom a building was being erected. There was some sense in this edict, for academics could be contentious and indecisive, and thereby slow up a project and add greatly to its cost. But the main result was to isolate the architect and to give him a spurious infallibility. It played into his desire to work out a design at the outset, to use what John Andrews calls an 'intuitive' approach and to impose it upon the basic users' requirements.

There was little chance that the University would change its policy on the main campus, where it was bound by the constrictions of the past and the ordinances of the city. But the decision to build a college on an entirely new campus, 20 miles from the old one, opened up new possibilities. Here was a chance to plan *ab initio*, to involve the users at every step, and, above all, to employ an architect who was not the slave of precedent. John Andrews was that architect; the man and the opportunity came together, and Scarborough College – the University's chapter in the history of modern architecture – was the result.

It was not easy to convince the governing body that John Andrews was the man for the job. He was young, unknown, with no visible record of achievement. Indeed his appointment, like the building itself, was more a 'happening', than an event. But the results were crucial for the University, for Andrews' career, and for modern architecture; and I rejoice in the part I played in bringing it about.

The methods Andrews used at Scarborough were followed in all his subsequent projects. He insisted upon a detailed analysis of the site and its relationship to the surrounding area. He kept human needs at the top of his scale of values and he never forgot that a building should not be a container for inert objects but a place where human beings move and work and play together. He reached his conclusions by perpetual dialogue with the users of the building – time-consuming it might seem, but ultimately a hedge against disaster.

This book gives you the flavour, and much of the substance, of those dialogues. The dialogues – or, more accurately, Andrews' summary of them – are preceded by formal analyses that put his building in the context of architectural history. The analyses are valuable and instructive, but the heart of the book is in the Andrews sections. They were taken down from tapes, and they preserve the peculiar and powerful Andrews rhetoric – a combination of sharp insights, scornful irony, and jolting humour, set in direct, colloquial language, with the great Australian expletive used with poetic gusto.

The book is a portrait of the artist as a young architect. Like all competent artists, Andrews began with a mastery of his craft. He became a great artist because he approached each problem with single-minded and passionate intensity and let the solution emerge naturally and inevitably from the pressure of the facts and the dictates of the imagination; or, to put the idea in Andrewsese, there was always 'an undeniable bloody logic to our concept'.

Claude Bissell

Introduction

This is a most reluctant book. I did not start out originally to write a book, but to record experiences which could be useful to students.

When teaching at the University of Toronto I became quite concerned that there was no part of the course where I could get students to understand the immense variety of experiences that go into building a building; and that the message a student gets about being an architect from a school of architecture is very much a false impression. The *nice* part of architecture, the creative art, which schools of architecture are all about, finally finishes up absorbing, at best, about one per cent of the time taken to complete any building.

The reluctance to record my experiences in book form was overcome initially by Earl Berger in Canada who began asking questions, taping answers and refining tapes into some sort of sense. That initial burst of energy died when I moved to Australia and away from the teaching world until regenerated some years later by Jennifer Taylor who picked up the story and insisted I finish it. In fact she plagued me to death. We agreed to fight the battle together, and I consider it full justice that besides writing the continuous text that appears in large face, she had to share the months (years) of agony recording and re-ordering my words for the individual building studies. The next task fell on my secretary Kathy Hampton who gallantly tackled the task of typing and retyping the manuscript.

It is important to understand that I have recorded, mainly when they occurred, a collection of impressions about particular buildings, about people, about times and places. The first drafts were made some 14 years ago and my text remains basically as I stated it then. I have resisted the temptation to alter my views as expressed at the time although, in retrospect and with the advantage of hindsight, I can maybe now see more clearly what should have happened. The task of translating spoken words into written words is almost impossible but I hope the conversational aspect of the words remains.

Throughout the following pages I have been as frank as is legally possible. In certain instances individuals may not be pleased with my reaction to them – a reaction, as I have said, which has likely changed over the years, but certainly was the way I felt at the time.

King George Tower, Sydney

M any words have been written as to whether architecture is an art or a science. Personally, I could not care less what it is called as long as *architecture* is the predominant word. I am often asked for my stated philosophy on architecture. Anybody who is interested in that will have to read this book which, I think, explains my various feelings about it, feelings not always consistent and certainly feelings which have not been the same over the last 10 to 15 years.

Passenger Terminal for the Port of Miami

Right *The Cameron Offices, Belconnen, Canberra*

I have not used the title *Architecture: A Performing Art* facetiously but as a play on the word 'performance'. The performance necessary to convince people to do what I believe will ultimately be good for them; performance in performing that other 99 per cent of producing a building, not much of it fun; performance, first of all in defining the problem, solving it sensibly, convincing other people of its appropriateness, documenting, wheeling and dealing, supervising and, above all, taking the responsbility – a responsibility that stays with an architect for the whole of his life with everything he builds; the performance of making sure you can survive under these circumstances which means fighting with builders, becoming more and more involved with the legal profession, paying insurance and trying to make sure you do not get wiped out by a decision that was maybe made by you, or maybe not, and made at some time long erased from your memory but for which you are still responsible. This performance is absolutely real and in these terms architecture is *certainly* a performing art.

Gund Hall, The Harvard Graduate School of Design, Cambridge

'He was the kind of architect the board so far had scrupulously avoided: young and inexperienced, and the board valued age and experience; contemptuous of the approach to building in terms of a specific style, and the board had a collective preference for homogenized Georgian; abrupt and unapologetic in his presentation of a scheme, and the board valued a smooth sales pitch. But at the same time they were impressed by Andrews: by his self-confidence and his unruffled boyish arrogance, by his easy grasp of detail and his swift response to practical needs.'

Claude Bissell
President of the University of Toronto
Halfway Up Parnassus, 1971

John Andrews
Architect

Response to challenge is the story of John Andrews' life, and for that matter, of his architecture. He was born in Sydney in 1933. Nothing short of determination and drive carried him to the University of Sydney, to Harvard, and then to Toronto. There he remained until 1969, when he returned to Australia to design the Cameron Offices, Canberra. His entry into the international forum of architecture was dramatic. In 1962, to his practice that consisted of kitchen renovations, was added the opportunity to design a new campus for the University of Toronto – Scarborough College. He was then twenty-nine. It was the architectural solution for this campus that suddenly brought Andrews' raw creative talent to the attention of the architectural world.

During the 1960s when the weaknesses of the polemics of the early modern movement were becoming increasingly evident, Andrews was among a handful of architects who attempted to grapple with the major issues generated by accelerating changing demands. Since that time he has designed a surprising number of significant, and sometimes controversial, buildings for North America and Australia. His buildings are rather like the man himself – confident and convincing. They are bold, rugged buildings that appear to rejoice in their involvement with the complexities of major environmental problems. Today, when intellectualizing is threatening to undermine common sense, the tough pragmatism in his architecture is one of its most welcome characteristics.

Two major themes are followed throughout his work; one is the search for a structured yet permissive urban order, the other a quest for solutions relevant to, and expressive of, social needs and aspirations. One surprising thing about Andrews is that while others theorize on the problem of architecture, he, in an almost intuitive way, recognizes the problem and produces a built solution. It appears to be a habit of his, that just when a theory is losing its conviction he comes up with a building that re-establishes its credibility.

The Andrews firm is made up of a small group of partners and employed architects. Convinced of the inappropriateness of a large bureaucratic structure, based on a hierarchy and designated levels of tasks, Andrews organized his office to consist of a small number of architects with shared responsibilities. Fifteen is seen as the optimum size, though due to fluctuations in work load the number varies. On one occasion it reached almost 30; but then contact and collaboration proved difficult.

The office is characterized by an informality which allows for flexibility in routine and time worked. The staff operates as a team, allowing each member of the firm to contribute from his own special area of interest and ability. Responsibility for any specific project is vested in a small group which then draws on the range of talents available. There is considerable reliance on outside consultants, brought in when their expertise is most needed. Andrews contends that co-operation between architect and builder is highly desirable during the design phase and whenever possible the builder is involved from this initial stage. Participation by the client is also demanded. This is made clear before the architectural contract is agreed upon, and those not prepared to contribute to the development of the project usually turn elsewhere. This loose framework requires a high level of communication and close affiliation between the project and all those involved in its design. The program itself is often radically revised to include what Andrews sees as 'enormously important design determinants that are not written down'.

Much of the success of the firm has resulted from the managerial practices that provide opportunity for creative input from all involved. Andrews remains the most influential partner. He capitalizes on his

forthright 'Australian' image, and enters the arena of clients, consultants and contractors with a purposeful logic, tempered by a sharp wit and tinged with a dramatic flair. He strongly believes in the validity of his architecture and has the tenacity to fight for its realization.

The starting point for the buildings lies in his definition of problems, ranging from universals to particulars. Scrutiny of the fundamental issues has given rise to the innovative nature of many of the projects. The pragmatism in his work is by nature rather than intent. He claims to hold no theory of architecture, and insists that architecture is neither an art nor science. 'It is just "architecture", and architecture is simply common sense' – a refreshing attitude that is contradicted by his own work.

Andrews is a most consistent architect. Experience based on past failures and successes has modified the shaping of spaces, and led to a refinement of structure, but his principles are constant, and variation in expression comes primarily from the nature of the specific task. Consequently there is a sequential development in the work rather than clearly defined changes in attitude and style. Ideas indicated in unbuilt projects, or hinted at in early buildings, are pursued until the opportunity for their full realization presents itself.

Within an overall conceptual framework the design evolves in a rational and systematic manner, with continual reference to the construction process. The expression of the building is pursued as a logical extension of the program. His strength here lies in an ability to manipulate forms into compatible orders, but, he claims, 'only the forms that start to want to happen'. While Louis Kahn's 'let a building be what it wants to be' is a basic tenet of his work, a nudge in the right direction at the right time allows the building to say what it wants to say. Yet there is a sense of inevitability in Andrews' architecture that is absent in Kahn's more formalized solutions.

Confidence in the assumptions on which the design was based is evident in the bold decisive statements of the built forms. To a remarkable extent the projects clearly express the principal issues that conditioned their development. Direct and uncompromising, they evidence the conflicts and contradictions which are simply accepted as part of the reality of the circumstances of architecture.

Steel frame of the Andrews House, Eugowra, New South Wales

The formal language, as with all who build in concrete, must inevitably relate to that of the early modern movement, and particularly to Le Corbusier. In this Andrews is no exception, and many of the devices he employs derive from the dynamic imagery of the mechanical preoccupation of that time. The Brutalist ethic is strongly expressed; yet raw materials, direct details, exposed structure and services derive not from a particular philosophical stance but 'because it makes sense'.

Perhaps more than those from any other designer today, his buildings show the development and realization of the planning theories that emerged following the dissolution of CIAM after the Otterlo Congress of 1959. Scarborough College, completed in 1965, was immediately recognized as the first built major statement of the concept of an open-ended lineal structure, organizing and relating functional units. The Bellmere Primary School of 1965, followed the centralizing yet expandable cellular matrix seen in Aldo van Eyck's Childrens Home, Amsterdam, and Louis Kahn's Trenton Bath House. Future projects, with few exceptions, adapt one or the other of these organizational patterns, with communication through circulation as the uniting theme.

Where possible the buildings are kept low and spread within a controlling geometrical structure to allow for diversity without disintegration. Particularly clear examples of this can be seen in the diagonal grid pattern of the Woden Offices Project and the lineal alignment of the Cameron Offices.

The Cameron Offices are more than a building; they are an element of an urban proposal. Even in the rural setting of the Scarborough College Andrews explored the urban situation. Open-ended, appearing incomplete, such structures appear as fragmentary parts indicating patterns for change.

Andrews' architecture is strongly conditioned by an intuitive response to human need, and his interpretation of suitable spaces and relationships to further personal and social well-being. In this respect his most challenging problems have arisen in attempting to provide identity for individuals in large-scale single-purpose schemes, such as the student residences for Guelph University and the offices for the Australian

Government at Belconnen. Contact with Aldo van Eyck and Herman Hertzberger is reflected in his attitude to design. The influence of their concepts of the nature of place and occasion, and of the universality of the fundamental human problems of design is evident in his words and his buildings.

With a commitment to architecture as the setting for human action and experience, he concentrates, in overall planning and in detail, on providing opportunity for communication between individuals, and between individuals and buildings. The importance he gives to circulation and informal areas arises from his understanding of the suitability of such spaces for social contact – movement becomes the primary generator of the physical and social framework. In contradistinction to 'beautiful object' architecture, these buildings without their occupants have a stark empty air like a deserted stage. Within their often seemingly deterministic forms the buildings are permissive – a strong architecture that can take the blows of change and use.

Andrews neither follows the establishment nor consciously leads revolutions. His buildings are set apart by his own personal commitment to the underdogs of architecture – the users; his insight into the problems of design from a particular perspective; and his ability to create a powerful imagery of architectural form. Because of these diverse attributes, Andrews' work often appears to exhibit a dichotomy between the genuine humanism of the implicit theory and the structured order and commanding presence of the explicit forms.

Andrews is a teacher as well as a designer. For him the issue is straightforward – simply 'learning how to solve problems'. This book sets forth how he saw, and in his own way, attempted to solve the problems of architecture. The problems were wide-ranging and involved issues that most architectural treatises prefer to pretend do not exist. He writes of architecture as a process, with success dependent on the architect's ability to perform well from the initial contact with the client through to the completion of the building – 'getting the thing built is a performance from beginning to end'. Andrews presents the creation of buildings as a series of confrontations, conflicting and co-operative. It appears here as more than a performance – a struggle from beginning to end.

Training and early projects

Andrews graduated from the Department of Architecture at Sydney University in 1956 equipped with five years of university training, office experience with the firm of Edwards, Madigan and Torzillo, and 'on-site' experience as a 'bush-builder' and on several houses of his own design (the whereabouts of which he refuses to disclose!). Perhaps his best learnt lessons were those forced upon him by circumstance. His father, a monumental mason, was deprived of his trade by the closure of his business during World War II, and for the rest of his life supported his family with money earned from a variety of manual jobs. Andrews had to be practical, to be able to improvise, and to make the most of every opportunity, while assisting his father in his work. During these years the attitude of some of his more affluent associates was not always easy to take. An early engendered feeling of resentment, and the determination to prove his own worth, explain much about the man and his achievements.

An education at North Sydney Boys' High School allowed him to enter the Department of Architecture at Sydney University with a strong background in the humanities, an ability 'to draw a bit', but an 'anathema for mathematics'. A shooting accident while in National Service led him to spend what would have been the second year of architecture in Concord Repatriation Hospital. In retrospect, Andrews sees this time as an ill wind that blew much good. Away from home for the first time and living with returned soldiers at Concord taught him 'a hell of a lot about how to perform and a hell of a lot more about people'. Between leaving hospital and re-entering the architecture course Andrews went 'bush building' as a builder's labourer. When the carpenter failed to arrive at the job he took over and for a short period was a member of the union. With this experience behind him he returned to the University.

During his time with Edwards, Madigan and Torzillo, the then small firm had few commissioned jobs and so Andrews was allowed to work on its entry for the Sydney Opera House Competition. Involvement in such a large-scale project was a rewarding experience for a student. A hidden benefit was the revelation of the wide range of solutions to the problem on which the office had been engaged for months – 'for the first time the possibilities of architecture became evident'.

With an honours pass from the University he gained entry to Harvard Graduate School of Design. The single living allowance for which he was eligible was a grant, offered every fifth year, that gave preference to the descendants of men totally incapacitated in World War I. His father was not thus afflicted, but, counting on the fact that there would not be too many graduating students whose fathers were, Andrews applied. Being the only candidate he won the award – a reward for resourcefulness as well as academic merit. He arrived in San Francisco with $40 in his pocket, but with the funds for the grant available once Harvard was reached.

The year spent at the Graduate School of Design was an enlightening period. Forced to think, forced to communicate, and exposed to the influence of such outstanding teachers and professional men as Sigfried Giedion and Josep Lluis Sert, Andrews felt he was at last on the way to becoming an architect. Under Dean Sert the emphasis in the School had changed from the strict Bauhausian line of Walter Gropius, towards the more expressive social and technological stance of the mature Le Corbusier. This was in marked contrast to the general direction of architecture in America which was aligned with the purity of Mies van der Rohe's language of steel and glass. Andrews' later work clearly demonstrates lessons well learnt at this time.

But there was little of Corbusier and much of Eero Saarinen in the project that first brought him to the attention of the architectural profession. In March 1958 Andrews and three American student colleagues submitted an entry to the Toronto City Hall International Competition. Although advised not to undertake the program, the four students moved into a rented basement room away from the school, set up drawing-boards, and worked on the project on a spare-time basis. Full of confidence and enthusiasm the group rented an eleven-bedroom home with a private beach and tennis court, on twenty-three acres of land at Cape Cod in anticipation of proceeding to Stage II of the competition! Their optimism was not misfounded – in October, the second stage was submitted.

Viljo Revell's winning entry from Finland consisted of two boomerang-shaped complimentary towers that cradled the lower council chambers and opened onto a large public plaza. The striking focus it provided came

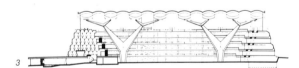

from the unconventional curving vertical forms and their height, which, at that time, provided a distinctive mark among the comparatively low-scale buildings of central Toronto. In contrast, the low-scale Harvard student entry relied on the formality of symmetry, and the exploitation of the pattern of the precast concrete wall panels and the intricate eye-catching curves of the umbrella roof system. The roof units supported elliptical sheets of glass in the vertical planes to permit light and sun to penetrate the heart of the complex.

The concept behind the outward show of the Harvard design revealed a regard for the climatic conditions of Toronto and the social role of a City Hall. The proposal included summer and winter plazas, an acknowledgement of the divergent seasonal characteristics, joined at the centrally-located council chambers. The summer plaza was seen as a great outdoor meeting-place; the sunlit winter plaza was covered by a huge roof, its wall formed by the surrounding government offices. These stepped back on the interior and were reached by open circulation balconies where the comings and goings of government activities were revealed. These balconies were also intended to provide grandstand views of events in the plaza below.

As a meeting-place for the citizens of Toronto, both as spectators and participants in many facets of civic affairs, the Harvard students' entry was a somewhat flamboyant yet sensitive solution. The near-success of the City Hall proposal led to an invitation from John B. Parkin, who eventually became Revell's Canadian associate, for Andrews to join the Toronto office of John B. Parkin Associates as senior designer. On the advice of Paul Rudolph, who had also offered him a position, he accepted the work in Toronto as it had more potential for design experience. In 1958 Andrews, now married, moved to Canada. The three years spent in the Parkin firm were to have lasting influence on his future attitudes.

At the age of 24, virtually penniless and straight from Harvard, it was difficult for Andrews to adjust to the tight hierarchical system of the Parkin firm. The structured levels of decision-making produced such an incompatible environment that eventually he retreated to the position of working on one solution for perusal and discussion by day, and his own solution by night – resulting in little but increased frustration. The fallacy

4

5

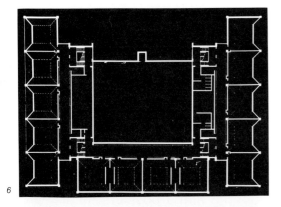

6

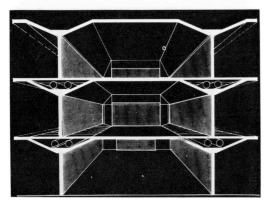

7

of these circumstances later conditioned the organization of his own office. As senior designer, in what was ostensibly an apprenticeship period with Parkin, Andrews was involved with the design of fairly large-scale projects. His work at this time showed a major concern for coping with the harsh Canadian climate; its effect both on the construction process and on the comfort of the buildings' users. Also evident in the regularity of the designs was the firm's persuasion towards the neoclassicism of Mies van der Rohe.

When building the Primrose Club, 1959, and the Federal Equipment Complex (now the Carruthers Building), 1959, a steel column and truss frame envelope was first erected to allow internal construction to proceed under controlled conditions. The full-storey deep trusses of the Primrose Club form a grid of enclosed rooms while the twin skylight-supporting trusses of the Equipment Complex are boxed in pairs and expressed externally. In both buildings the envelopes enclose simple, orderly spaces. Changes to the initial design have transformed the Primrose Club into what appears as a badly proportioned classical composition, giving little hint of the rationale behind its design.

The introverted Saulte Ste Marie Secondary School, also of 1959, shows a further response to the harsh climatic conditions of Canada. The planning was related to that of Kahn's Trenton building, with individual two- and three-level classroom units wrapped around the central gymnasium and general utility spaces. The concrete 'tent' slabs, monolithically connected to column supports, provides a relatively light, fireproof structure suitable for the soft foundation bed. This structural system allows for the integration of services and provides overhangs against the glare from snow-covered ground. The repetitive use of three standard steel forms for the 34 tent structures of the building enabled speedy construction and a high level of control over the concrete finishes.

Two further designs for Parkin Associates show the ideas and techniques that were established as Andrews' work at this time. The concept of removing the central core of a large office building and dividing its functions into three separate peripheral towers, acting both as service and support, can be seen in a project for an office building of 200 000 square feet for prime tenancy in downtown Toronto. The resulting

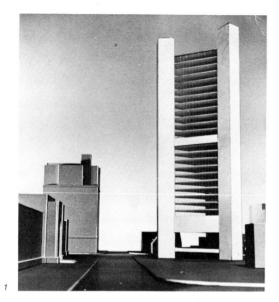

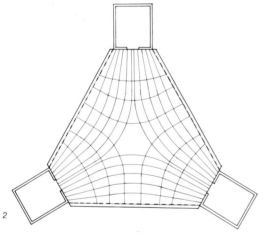

triangular plan form with divorced points of entry allows three office units to operate independently on each level. Designed much later, King George Tower, Sydney, now American Express Tower, shows a similar organization that arose from quite different considerations.

This basic arrangement also appeared in a modified version for the Malton Control Tower of Toronto Airport. The design for Malton Tower carried the related services of stairs, elevators and ducts in its three supports, and formed the central focus to the low level, axially arranged units that sustained its operation. It was the obvious forerunner to the preliminary three-legged design for the Canadian National Tower, Toronto.

It was with the proposed design for the Malton Hotel at Toronto Airport that Andrews took the major step towards the approach that typifies his work today. Rather than working against the various constraints that impinge on the building design he began to work with them. The forms were generated in response to the conflict between sleeping accommodation, and the location, directly under the approaches to the main runway and alongside a six-lane highway. The bedrooms were arranged around three courts serving specific major functions. As the plan form increased in size from unit to unit, so did the building height and in this way conformed to the inclined building height limit dictated by the runway approaches. Concrete load bearing construction, single corridors and enclosed balconies created barriers against noise in the individual rooms. A five-foot projection of each superimposed level provided further sound protection. The resulting sloping forms surrounding the courts would have helped to deflect sound waves and to eliminate the reverberation that would have occurred between vertical enclosures. The staggered section reappeared in his later major designs for Scarborough College, Gund Hall and the Cameron Offices.

With the Malton Hotel project, Andrews broke from the formal influence of Saarinen and Mies. Virtually the antithesis of Saarinen's poetry of flight in the wings of the TWA Terminal, New York, the forms of the Malton Hotel design express the realities of airport conditions. For the first time he demonstrated his ability to communicate the relevance of his solution. During the time spent at Parkin Associates Andrews developed an awareness of the functional and expressive potential of resolved structures, and of orderly and logical design concepts. The Malton Hotel program reveals a fresh insight.

In 1961 Andrews embarked on an 'architectural pilgrimage' to Europe, Russia, the Middle East and India. Revell, with whom he worked on the structural redesign of the City Hall at the end of his time with Parkin, guaranteed the financial loan that made the trip possible. Disappointment with most of the 'masterpieces' of modern architecture was balanced by an increase in his own confidence for he felt, with notable exceptions, that 'they really weren't all that hot after all'. The rationality of Corbusier's seemingly non-functional forms at Ronchamp, and the sensitivity of Gaudi's blending of natural forms and passages for movement at Parc Güell did not go unnoticed. But for Andrews the vernacular architecture was more rewarding and enlightening – not so much the beauty of form, but the plain logic behind solutions that were obviously suitable for their location and use – 'Just marvellous simple ideas – the water wells in India that are just a series of stairs so that as the water recedes you can still get at it, and the lightweight covers across the top that provide shade'. The environments that resulted from the application of the well-intentioned lore of the modern movement were found lacking when mentally juxtaposed with the eminently satisfying environments created by a practical rather than a theoretical stance. This reinforced what he already believed to be the most valid approach to architecture.

Before returning to Canada, four months were spent in Sydney in the office of Stephenson and Turner, a firm noted primarily for hospital designs. Declining an invitation to return to the Sydney firm, he spent some time in Montreal and then settled in Toronto. The Andrews family moved into the top floor of a house in Woodlawn Avenue, occupied by Richard Strong, a landscape architect who had joined Parkin's firm in 1959. Both occupants were foundation members of a five-man group called INTEG ('Integrated Professions' as it consisted of an engineer, an accountant, a lawyer, a landscape architect and an architect) which had purchased the property in 1960. The engineer was Norbert Seethaler, who had worked with Andrews on his designs for the Parkin firm.

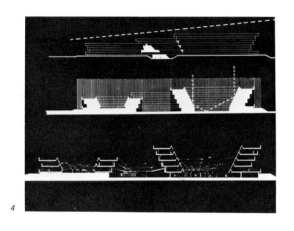

4

1 Office building for Toronto
2 Flat slab stress diagram for the triangulated office building for Toronto
3 Model, Malton Control Tower
4 Malton Hotel project showing the effect of considerations of sound factors on the building form

The INTEG group bought an empty warehouse in Colborne Street and moved their offices into the old building. Andrews' own practice consisted of an unbuilt proposal for a shopping centre, kitchen renovations, and some model-making for more successful practices. His practice income was supplemented by part-time teaching at the Architecture Department of the University of Toronto. Reaction to what he saw as the inadequacy of his own training at Sydney University, particularly the absence of any purposeful exchange between staff and students, strongly conditioned Andrews' attitude to education. A full-time appointment as Assistant Professor later provided the first chance to put forward his ideas on architectural education. Among Andrews' future partners were several who were students in the department at this time.

The 1960s were progressive years for Canadian architecture. Financial prosperity enabled exploration for fresh solutions to the old and new problems of building. The outcome was a wave of imaginative answers that arose from a thorough reassessment of elementary questions and answers. A common feature of many of the new designs was the use of internal pedestrian circulation zones. At the same time these buildings reached outside the confines of their site to unite the structure with the forms and activities of the surroundings. Andrews' Canadian work belongs in the vanguard of this creative upswing.

But in 1962 while the economy and the building industry boomed, Andrews' practice did not. In August that year however, he was asked if he would be interested in joining a planning team to evolve the master plan for a new satellite college for the University of Toronto at Scarborough. He was.

North America:
Scarborough
Bellmere
Guelph
African Place
Miami
Metro Centre
Gund Hall

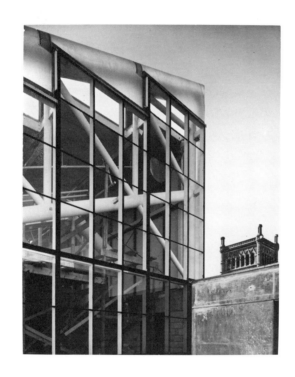

Breakthrough

Six years is not a long time in which to transform a practice dependent on model-making into one of international stature. But that is what Andrews achieved in Canada. It would not be a mean feat for anyone, but for a 29-year-old Australian with little support of any kind, it was quite an astounding performance.

Scarborough College presented a not-to-be-missed opportunity. In an all out burst of intensive work, Andrews, Michael Hough, a landscape architect, and Michael Hugo-Brunt, an architect-planner, charged through and beyond the required outline master plan. At the end of six weeks they presented not a preliminary analysis but a design proposal. Impressed by the performance, the Board of Governors appointed Andrews as architect in association with the large firm of Page and Steele.

Scarborough College is remarkable in many respects, but its outstanding characteristic is the spontaneous vigour evident in its design. Andrews never has and never will produce another Scarborough College. Raw and unstudied, the building has the exuberance and directness of its genesis. With little time to meditate or theorize, the problems were grasped, defined and solved as they arose. The collection of powerful forms rises courageously from the determinants. From the site Andrews drew the dramatic ridge and allowed the building to follow its contours. The fine stands of maples and beeches on the adjacent slopes remained untouched and the building rears over them like a fortress. The enclosed connecting street system provided not only a shelter from the extremes of the Toronto climate, but a dramatic expression of the major design theme. Andrews' belief in the role of a building as a generator for social exchange underlies the general planning. The spaces and forms of the various sections arose from the specific nature of the teaching program, but the richness of the variety of the individual parts of Scarborough come from the acceptance and expression of the accord and discord in that program. Scarborough changed on site – adjusting itself as problems arose, accepting the realities of construction. Consequently, the building illustrates a relationship between building methods and detailed design and decoration, as in the craft tradition.

Chimney stack, Scarborough College

While designed for growth along the ridge, planning changes resulted in the location of Stage II close to the centre of the complex. The restrained design of the completed Stage II extension, by John Simpson, who later became a partner in the office, while not furthering the initial concept, respects what was originally there.

Scarborough gave credence to the widespread theories of the time, that a memorable image could emerge from an architecture that celebrated the construction process and the functional requirements of its spaces. Scarborough is not a series of buildings related along a circulation spine; it totally rejected the then conventional idea of a building as an element with a recognizable independent existence. It is a continuous structure within which circulation is elevated to a symbolic level.

In massive monolithic concrete, Scarborough's parts certainly could not be altered, but it is an intentionally unfinished structure that represents an attitude towards, rather than the reality of, a building's acceptance of the demands of growth and change.

Stage IIA extensions

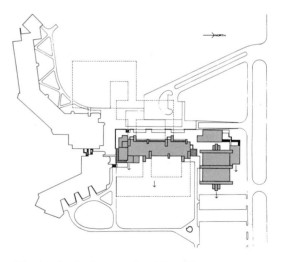

Site plan showing the expansion of Stage IIA

The summer of 1962 I was broke, with virtually no practice. Thomas Howarth, Chairman of the University of Toronto School of Architecture, invited me to come on the staff part-time as a design critic for fifth year students. The salary was $3000, which was more than I was making anywhere else. I liked the work and by second term, having no other work to do, I was spending most of my time at the school. Michael Hough, who was teaching landscape architecture part-time and acting as landscape architect to the University, was asked to whip up a quick site plan for the land the University had purchased in the Borough of Scarborough for a satellite college. To his eternal credit Hough had the good sense to realize this was no way to go about developing a new campus. He persuaded the University to retain him, Michael Hugo-Brunt, a planner, and myself as the master planning team for Scarborough College.

The program consisted of a Users' Report on area requirements related to teaching needs prepared by faculty members assisted by the University's physical plant staff. Our task was to develop a master plan for the College, with an initial student enrolment of 1500, rising to 5000 (with the possibility in our minds that the number might increase in a decade or two to the point where the College would become a separate university). The total stipulated area was 213 000 square feet with a budget of $6.3 million. We subsequently proved that the facilities set out in the Users' Report would require 400 000 square feet in order to work. The report had omitted space allocations for a number of ancillary requirements such as storage, circulation and space for the large television complex, and had not included in the budget sums for site services. The difference between the budgeted and real cost of the college can be attributed largely to these major omissions.

Work began in the summer of 1963. The Board of Governors was in the summer recess. This meant the Chairman, the Vice-Chairman and the President, Claude Bissell, had the summer option to carry on as the full Board, a tool the Chairman liked to use when he wanted to

move things quickly. It was much easier to work informally with these three men than with a full Board. The three combined the qualities of enthusiasm, imagination and hard-nosed practicality which allowed us scope for innovation yet still kept us within realistic limits.

Working directly with us was Carl Williams, Principal-Designate of the College, and William Beckel, an assistant professor of zoology who had worked on the Users' Report. Beckel was in town for the summer and offered to lend a hand. I was a firm of two, myself and Jim Sykes. Jim, a superb craftsman and graduate architect with a lake-boat master's certificate, had appeared at Colborne Street one day when I had no money to hire anybody and no work for them to do. He decided to work for me without salary until I could afford to pay him. He built models and supervised kitchen renovations for months until there was enough money from Scarborough College to pay him.

I took Ed Galanyk on to the staff and all of us, including William's secretary, moved into the University's old Chemistry Building, prior to its demolition. We put in some drawing-boards, tacked up some bulletin boards and that became the Scarborough College Planning Office. The essential factor was that we were all together in one place. We could contact the key decision-maker, Williams, or his faculty advisor, Beckel, as often as we wanted by walking a few feet through the door into their office. The planning team was organized so that the landscape architect and planner acted as resources to the architect, providing background data which Galanyk and I tried to synthesize into something which made sense. This was the right time and place for myself, Williams and Beckel. We were all hungry as hell. I was boiled up and frustrated with a practice that was not giving me the kind of work I had spent years preparing myself for. I was busting to take a problem like Scarborough College and tackle it in a rational, common sense way. My involvement was accidental, but the opportunity was real. I had to take it as far as I could.

The timing was critical. Normally the University would allow four years for the planning and development of a major building. We had 25 months in which to plan, design and build a college for 1500 students. Only six weeks were allocated for the master plan.

It is usual to spend some two or three weeks simply working out how best to tackle a problem. There was no time for that at Scarborough, and not much experience. Things got done as they happened to come up, not in any logical sequence; everything was one big jumble. Even the academic program was unique in that a basic requirement was television teaching. No one had ever done that before in Canada. The only people we could talk to were Williams and Beckel. As a group we were on our own.

Carl Williams, Director of the University's extension program, had been given his own college. He was enthusiastic, committed to creating something outstanding and determined not to let anyone cut us down. He ran most of the political interference for us – of which I was largely ignorant at the time. Perhaps we were wrong to keep the bureaucrats away but we had no time to muck about with endless committees and meetings, or to pay obeisance to everyone's little empire. Beckel received no official designation from the University until later but for all practical purposes it made no difference. If we agreed on something it was difficult for anyone to shoot it down – especially since we had only six weeks in which to do the master plan.

The pressure created by the limitations of time was enormous. The one advantage was that the University was a bit embarrassed at the schedule they had given us. If we had no time for leisurely second thoughts, the University could not hold us up by wasteful bureaucratic procedures and delays in decision-making. Throughout the entire project the one thing which enabled us to meet our time-limits were the people representing the client: intelligent, committed, quick off the mark and not afraid to make decisions. With that an architect can do anything.

The problem

The site was the problem. I am sure it was chosen because of its beauty; 202 acres of wooded ravine and hillside, part of a larger ravine network running through the metropolitan area. In the valley were beautifully manicured grounds with the remains of a nine-hole golf course, a croquet ground and a river. Add a few stone buildings and you could have had an instant 200-year-old Ivy League campus.

In more important ways the site made no sense. It was located in a thinly settled suburb, far from the densely developed areas where the students lived. There was no public transport worth mentioning, no commercial facilities and the available housing was standard suburban detached, totally incapable of accommodating any appreciable number of students. There was no time to get into an argument about the suitability of the location. You had to tell your conscience that the new College would act as a catalyst, that it would be big enough to attract public transport facilities, commercial facilities, and other ancillary development. On the plus side was the extraordinary visual appeal of the immediate surrounds.

We began an intensive site analysis. Hugo-Brunt discovered that the Metropolitan Toronto Conservation Authority had passed a regulation that all ravine development had to occur on or over the brow so that the floors would remain available for public use. The University at that time had sufficient expropriation powers to overrule this regulation and build its ancient campus, but we were already uneasy about the ravine floor as a building site.

Hough had brought in Professor F. B. Watts, a climatologist. I cannot pretend to have had enough nous at that time to realize the contribution a climatologist could make, but his data turned out to be vital. He found that the ravine floor was unsuitable for buildings. The amount of sun the valley received was reduced by the edges of the ravine. At night the cold air would lie in the valley floor because of the action of katabetic winds caused by the local gravitation of cold air down the steep slope. Hough also discovered a marsh in the valley. My reaction was, if it is a marsh let us fill it in and make a playing field. But Hough reported that by an accident of drainage this was a pure marsh, unpolluted, and a valuable teaching tool. It was important to leave it in its natural state.

With this information we were able to convince the University they should not contemplate any building on the ravine floor. Playing fields would not be used at night when there might be a climate problem and could be located so as not to interfere with the Metro Conservation Authority's plan for a continuous public green area throughout the ravine network or the natural marsh areas.

The college from the ravine

We were then left with 39 acres at the top of the ravine to work with. The climatologist found that this site, because it was exposed to the winds off nearby Lake Ontario, had a winter chill factor of 15 to 20 degrees lower than that in the city proper. He also found that out of the six possible locations on the site, the best climatic location was on the edge of the northern ravine hill. It was here that the climate could most easily be controlled. The site faced south and slightly west. A building along the edge would cut off the winds and weather from the north and minimize the effect of drifting snow. Also the south-facing slope received two and one-half times more energy from the sun than did the other possible locations.

Seemingly minor matters kept turning into major planning determinants. One of the site's outstanding characteristics was the substantial amount of indigenous tree growth. We were interested in keeping as many trees as possible. At the same time you cannot cavort a building all over hell's half acre to miss a few trees. Some line had to be drawn between what should be kept and what could be replaced. Hough discovered some beautiful American beeches well over 100 years old and you have to think a bit more before hacking those down than you do a few maples. The beeches became a design determinant. Hough and I had some strong confrontations over what was expendable.

The master plan

The formulative concept was Scarborough College as a small Canadian town. With 5000 students or more, and several hundred faculty and administrative personnel the College would have the population of a village. We did not think at that time that the College population would be large enough to support a complex of streets, intersections, back lanes and squares typical of a city, but we were confident it would support one major circulation route with the major activities – formal and informal, business and pleasure – located along it. The 50 minute lecture/10 minute change time ratio generated a definitive time and distance relationship between all facilities and largely determined the physical bounds of the complex. Considering the size of the site we were working with, and the climate, it seemed unrealistic to proceed with a conventional master plan consisting of individual buildings scattered over 39 acres. The students would spend five or six months, almost the full academic year, stumbling through wind, rain, sleet and snow, from building to building, fumbling with coats and galoshes, getting wet, cold and ill. It seemed much more sensible to connect all the buildings. Once that was decided upon, we were involved with something quite different from the usual outdoor university circulation system. More than climate was involved in the development of the concept of an enclosed pedestrian

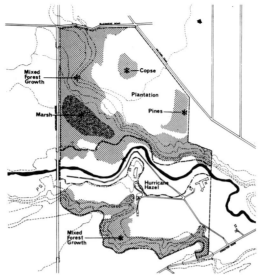

Existing landscape material

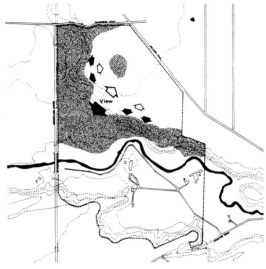

Naturally available views

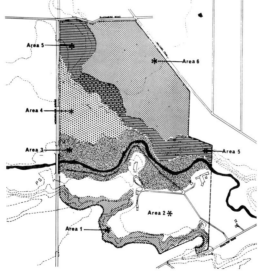

Climatalogical zones

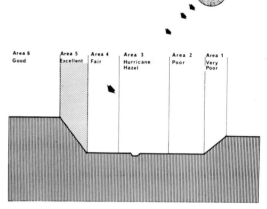

Section showing climatalogical zones

circulation system. What Corbusier had done at Marseilles was a street in the air with no logical beginning or end, a route arrived at by elevator with a few shops plugged into it. It had none of the rationale or common sense of the small town main street. Our approach was to provide a ground level interior pedestrian circulation route with high use destinations plugged into it, and secondary routes above and below it.

A university as a learning environment does not consist solely of the formal academic learning spaces. Learning occurs in the informal places in which people meet; the circulation system, the lounges, the cafeterias and other communal facilities. Our intent was to increase the effectiveness of these informal learning spaces. The enclosed circulation system gave us the opportunity to provide a climate-controlled college campus in which informal, as well as formal, learning could occur regardless of the weather.

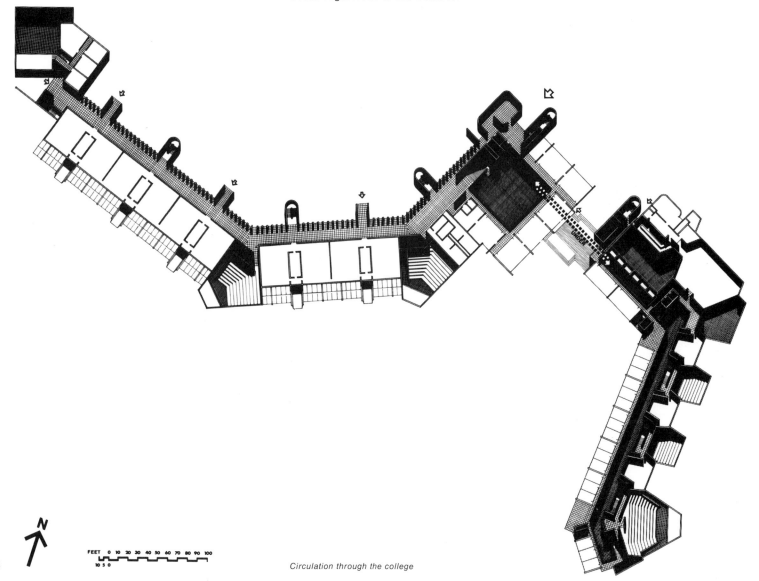

FEET 0 10 20 30 40 50 60 70 80 90 100
      10 5 0

Circulation through the college

The street thus becomes the main artery of the College. With the building sitting on the edge of the ravine it did not take much analysis to discover an additional benefit. We could put two levels above grade and two below, and still keep the building operating as a two-storey pedestrian environment. It also meant that we had a five-storey space with no need for elevators except for service. The master plan proceeded on this basis, using the site as resourcefully as possible.

The site was a strong one, bending and turning along the edge of the ravine. Soil surveys showed a fault in the middle of the site; slippage had already occurred making it unwise to build there. The building had to kick back from the edge of the ravine at this place thereby creating in a natural way a flat area open to the sun from the south and protected by the building from the wind and weather from the north. The bowl effect would collect and hold the sun and warmth, and the view was extensive. This was the most sensible place to put student lounges and cafeterias, and the administration offices where people sit all day in one place and need a view.

Sewers are notoriously expensive to build and it seemed reasonable to put the major sewer user as close to the existing municipal pumping plant as possible to keep site costs down. This meant that the Science Building had to be closest to the plant.

Given these climate and site factors, we knew we would have a wall-like building moving along the edge of the ravine, made up of three major components: science, administration and humanities.

Also, we wanted to develop a university environment out of this isolated moose pasture, something with which the first students arriving could identify, something complete in itself, something which would not have to be continuously hacked up and changed totally to handle increased enrolment. The building had to handle expansion without disturbing those learning and other activities which already existed. Existing built-form

imposes limitations on what can be added to it. A major conceptual requirement was to cut these limitations to the absolute minimum. Whatever the changing content of education, the technology of learning and teaching, whatever the new machinery – and no one could forecast what any of these would be – they had to be accommodated in succeeding stages of expansion. The answer to all these requirements was something which could be added to at either end at any time with increments which could take whatever shape or space was necessary to handle the needs of the time.

The buildings of the initial stage were to form the central college space, a formal hub of activity, with the Administration Building at centre flanked by the Science Building on one side and the Humanities Building on the other. Each building was to be complete in itself, from the time it first opened, including all its eating and communal facilities. All buildings could be entered by an interior pedestrian street from the central space. This allowed academic activities to remain undisturbed during the construction of the ensuing phases and construction to proceed unimpeded by the teaching function.

Site plan showing the original proposal for future expansion

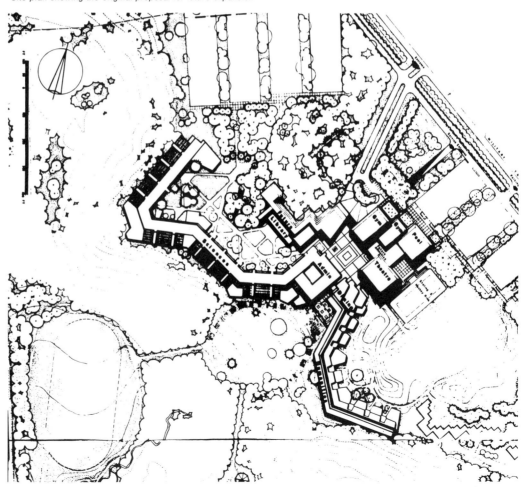

The Administration Building, unlike the others, was to be built to its final size in the first phase. The unused higher floors would be occupied by the College Library until it was built in a following phase.

The central location of the Administration Building allowed for the creation of a separate service level below grade so that all service activities could be separated and concealed from the pedestrian circulation system. The separation of circulation was extended to exterior spaces. Service vehicles were provided with their own access road into the College below ground level. Cars were restricted to the periphery of the campus, the furthest parking point being not more than a 10 minute walking distance from the central space. In this way, the main campus and its spaces were left free for pedestrian movement without conflict with vehicles.

This description of the master planning process may give the impression we were working in a planned, co-ordinated, sequential way. We were not. There were not all sorts of wonderful ideas to sift through in a logical manner, or run through a computer to obtain the statistical comparisons. With only six weeks, everything came in at once in a jumble, everything was ass-backwards, there were no definitive authorities to rely upon, most of what I did I sucked out of the end of my thumb. I was convinced, though, that all these problems had a common sense answer, as long as we concentrated on trying to find it we would produce a sensible solution. Common sense by this time in my career overtook any preconceived notions of form.

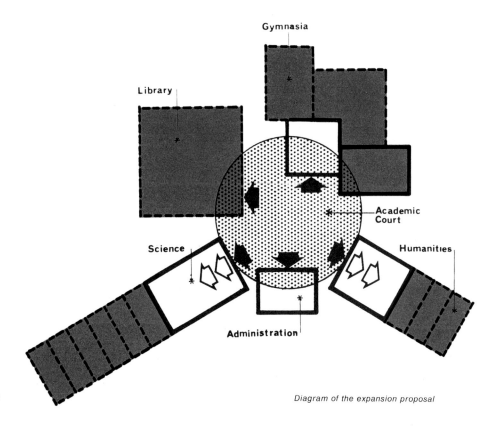

Diagram of the expansion proposal

Aerial view

At the end of six weeks it was time to present the results to the Board of Governors. When I first arrived at the University I was almost totally inarticulate; the idea of speaking in public was beyond my imagination. Working with students as critics had loosened me up to the degree that I now could manage a few words in sequence. But this was my first meeting with the Board of Governors and there was not a lot holding me in one piece when I stood up to speak. That presentation *was* architecture as a performing art.

There was an eight foot by ten foot flow pen drawing showing the basic concepts of the total plan, a site model, models showing sections of the Science and Humanities Buildings, and 25 or 30 sheets showing relevant aspects of town planning impact, site analysis, microclimate, drainage, master planning concepts, circulation. These were arranged in sequence, building logically to our solution. The models and diagrams were

covered with sheets, and as we progressed from stage to stage of our reasoning the appropriate diagram or model was uncovered with a flourish. Finally it was time to uncover the models of the buildings. All the Board members rose to their feet at once, just as if they had been tipped in the air, to have a look. Colonel Phillips, Chairman of the Board, who was not noted for being generous with his words – he was a tough old bastard as I recall – said, 'Gentlemen, the presentation leaves me not unmoved'. That was it. The presentation was over.

The solution
What the University needed at this point was a real architect to design the college, not some young guy screwing around with a master plan. I was a nobody, without experience on large projects. The University also needed someone to tell them if, in fact, the master plan was feasible.

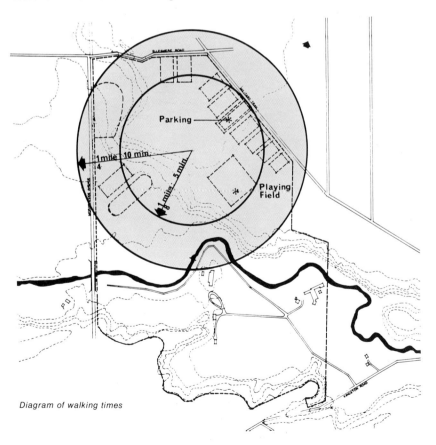

Diagram of walking times

The firm selected was Page and Steele, Architects, a large firm not known for innovative work. In the final analysis Williams and Beckel were prepared to fight for the implementation of the master plan but they would have had a great deal of trouble defending it if Page and Steele had said it was unrealistic.

When selecting Page and Steele, the University stipulated that Robert Anderson, a junior partner in the firm, be partner-in-charge of the project as he had proven his ability to bring complex projects in on time and budget with the Galbraith Engineering Headquarters at Toronto University. I had never met Anderson before. But he was a good, straight man who saw something in the master plan. He told Page and Steele categorically they would not design it, I would. They agreed and a joint venture resulted.

A Design Committee was established by the University. I represented design, Anderson represented production, Williams and Beckel represented the College, and Frank Hastie, director of the University's physical plant department, represented the janitocracy – or so I thought. Years later I recognized the contribution Hastie made to the project and to me. He insisted the work be done on university premises instead of at Page and Steele where I would have been swamped. He specifically ordered many of his janitocracy to leave us alone. In doing so, he took a tremendous responsibility on his own shoulders. At one point, the Board of Governors decided to cancel the project and he personally was under the gun, but he stuck by us. All I knew at the time was that I was going to build that bloody building to the design. The Design Committee met once a week and dealt with all matters relating to design and design implementation. Anyone with pet peeves had to go through it; there was no politicking on the outside.

Even before the architects had been selected the University had chosen its engineers for the project; a large multi-service firm which had as a senior partner the recently retired

chairman of Civil Engineering from the University. The choice of one, total-service engineering firm was probably made in good faith. On paper such a firm should provide significant benefits in terms of improved communications and co-ordination. Unfortunately, it worked out quite differently. The work by individual members of the firm was often first-rate. However, anything requiring co-operative action amongst the departments failed because of inter-departmental rivalry and the lack of organizational structure for integrated operations.

After the master plan was presented and accepted, the next three or four months were spent redesigning the Humanities Building and making presentations to all the necessary authorities. It was the Fall of 1962 and the College had to be open by September 1964. Anderson decided to combine design with construction management tied together by a critical path network as a means of speeding up the design-implementation process. A critical path network is a sequential diagram of activities. He also wanted to get started with a contractor before the University decided to bring in management consultants to run the operation. Consultants were hired to develop a critical path network and a management contract approach with sequential tendering.

The critical path network drawn up by Anderson and his consultants looked like a cavalry charge; everything had to happen at once. The very idea of the critical path scared me to death but I finally realized there was no other way to get through in time. Critical paths had been used before this, but to the best of my knowledge never on a project comparable in size to Scarborough College, and certainly never on anything but the construction process itself. Anderson deserves a tremendous amount of credit for realizing that the network had to reach back to the activities of the architect in the design phase, but yet not control them.

The contractor was a key man. By abandoning the traditional method of lump sum tendering

in favour of sequential tendering we could retain the contractor as a professional consultant. For a stipulated fee he worked with the architects and engineers during the design and working drawing phases as a consultant on buildability and cost. During the construction phase he was responsible for letting out tenders in sequence to meet the schedule and for managing the sub-trades involved.

Finding a contractor able to meet the necessary criteria was a complicated process. He had to have the financial and physical resources to spend a million dollars a month during construction. He had to be expert with concrete. Steel frame construction was out of the question as all the basic decisions have to be made before the steel can go up. With concrete, by pouring excessive footings and leaving other margins, we could move in stages, dealing with each problem as it arose.

Out of the ten firms which met the basic criteria, eight expressed an interest in the project. Each was given a set of outline drawings and other information and asked to state how they would handle the job, the time involved, and the name and experience of the job superintendent, concrete foreman and other key staff. No mention was made of money.

On the basis of the replies, four firms were selected, any one of which we would have been happy to work with. They had the resources, the right people and the right attitude to us and to giving the job a heave ho to get it in on time. Each of these firms was then asked to tender on the fee as a percentage of overall cost and the percentage of labour burden for their own construction work. The E. G. M. Cape Co. had the lowest bid and won the contract.

Cape were not in the usual position of being committed to a lump sum tender and having to realize their profit out of the difference between the tender price and what they could save on

the job itself. They were making their fee whatever was built; therefore their concern was for the building – not their pocketbook.

Working with the contractor, not against him, was a great experience. We were allies, not enemies. I was able to call on his expertise in building, which was a lot more than mine. Scarborough College was innovative from the earliest conceptual stage right through the construction phases to completion. The dialogue with the contractor during building and detailed design phases was as important as the dialogue with the academics during the conceptual and design phases.

Because of the shortage of time we desperately needed to eliminate the conventional procedure of communication by mail between consultants. What was needed were the theoretical benefits of the total service firm with none of the actual drawbacks. We rented the fifth floor of the School of Architecture during summer recess and put everyone in there, including Williams and Beckel. At times there were 30 or 40 people at work. Only three or four were from Page and Steele who were too busy with other projects to provide more staff. To make up the difference we hired summer students from fifth year, graduate students and some young architects. They were tremendous, bright, dying to get their teeth into something good and willing to work with a dedication hard to get from a man who has been through the mill for 10 years and wants to get home by 6 o'clock every night. Like everything else about Scarborough, the presence of these young architects was sheer luck. They had a great deal to do with resolving the detailed design. With a more mature and less enthusiastic staff the results would have been very different. A relationship, which began then, still continues today with one of these young architects, John Simpson, from Scotland.

Even before the master plan was presented to the Board of Governors for approval it was clear the Humanities Building had to be rethought. The section was wrong, not responding strongly enough to site and

41

exposure conditions. The lecture theatre opened up to the main interior street and to the sun, but the offices faced both north and south.

The offices were reorganized to face only to the south. The building is now like an animal turning its back to the northern weather. Moving up from level to level the offices step out to provide their own sunshade. Inside, the offices open on to interior streets which create a natural cross-ventilation system that eliminates the need for air-conditioning. In all respects the section is much more resourceful than in the preliminary design.

The Users' Report specified that there be no windows in the science laboratories in order that all the wall space could be used for displays, charts and equipment. Our reply was that this meant all the walls should be used for services, not that there should be no windows. The architectural solution was skylights. Unless there is a strong requirement for blackout – and even then, as we discovered with the lecture theatres – a space with no visual connection to the outside is rarely wanted. The connection might be distant, but it should be sufficient to allow the inhabitants to determine whether it is day or night, sunny or rainy. Starting with windowless walls we ended up with a stepping-back form for the Science Building to allow for skylights at each level. There was not, as some people seem to believe, any desire to imitate the Aztecs; the concept derived directly from the problem of providing natural light to the labs, yet retaining full wall space.

This approach to planning was unreal to many university people. They had never used anything like it before. People from the superintendent's office had nothing useful to say about the specific problem of natural light; they simply objected that the skylights would leak, therefore no skylights. We won that fight and, of course, the skylights did leak – not because they were skylights but because of the way they had been constructed. It was the manufacturer's problem and was eventually corrected.

With a closed circuit television facility there was no need to build the traditional, cumbersome hundred-man laboratory. These were replaced with twenty-man laboratories; twenty is a good number for group learning, can be handled by one instructor and can comfortably watch a moderately priced television receiver. This arrangement afforded an opportunity for multiple use of space. Single-use spaces are an expensive factor in the capital and operating costs of a university. The economy we sought was not minimal quality but a fundamental organization of spaces which would allow them to be used intensively for a reasonably broad range of activities.

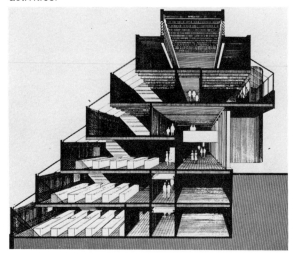
Section, science wing

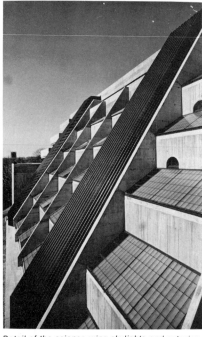
Detail of the science wing skylights and exterior mechanical ducts

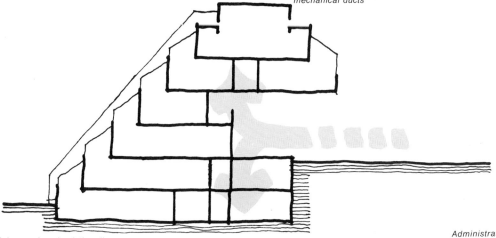
Science wing circulation diagram

Administration

The humanities program established a requirement for a large number of seminar rooms. The many small science laboratories gave the science faculty more flexibility in the programming and scheduling of courses and also gave the humanities faculty access to seminar-sized rooms for their purposes.

To the extent possible within the time available, most space usages were analyzed and treated in a similar way. Although Scarborough College is generously endowed with circulation and informal meeting places, it has an overall space utilization efficiency of 73 per cent; the best the University of Toronto had achieved until then was approximately 60 per cent.

To make the science laboratories work as seminar spaces, it was necessary to rethink and redesign the conventional laboratory furniture and fixtures. Instead of the usual continuous trough with the black marble edge, we developed small independent stations with retractable service pods between students. Tables and chairs were provided instead of stools and benches. No one could suggest an ideal furniture arrangement to meet the different needs of the users, so the furnishings were left loose for the faculty and students to shuffle around as they wished.

There was a tremendous problem getting the University to approve comfortable furniture for the student lounges and sitting areas. The University insisted on something non-slashable. We threatened to give the students some of the slashable variety ourselves. Finally the University agreed that the majority of people, even students, do not slash furniture, and there is nothing seriously wrong if the occasional person takes the odd slash or two. They will get over it if no one makes a big fuss. To date the padded couches and chairs have been in use at the college for 14 years and, so far as I know, not one has been slashed. Like anybody else, students are reasonably competent to look after possessions they like so long as others do not surround them with meaningless, humiliating rules.

43

The mechanical services were extracted out of the building, not to imitate the manifold of a Stutz Bearcat, but in order to establish a sensible relationship between structure and services. It would have been foolish to riddle the Science Building, for example, with vertical service ducts, each of which would have had to be so big you could drive a ten-ton truck through it. Located outside the building, the service ducts are out of the way, covered by a tin lid and easily accessible. The popular talk about the integration of mechanical services and structure is nonsense. Structure cannot change; it holds up the building. Mechanical services can, and undoubtedly will, change over time. If men can live in a space capsule without the standard bulky boiler plant and air-conditioner, it is certain that mechanical services for buildings will eventually catch up with this technology. The mechanical services have to be arranged to be able to accommodate these changes.

In the Humanities Building this approach gave us an interesting effect. It is difficult to take a square stepping out on four sides and turn a corner with it. Getting the mechanical service ducts to their positions under the windows also turned out to be a nice architectural way of getting around the corner – as well as keeping the service ducts outside and easily accessible.

A minor piece of detailed design took us right to the heart of the matter of what a university, and particularly Scarborough College is about; it is the microcosm of a small town, and as such it must provide the same opportunity for continuing social contact as is provided by a town.

In many universities, however, the opportunity for continuing contact between undergraduates on the one hand, and graduates and faculty on the other is unavailable. The latter depend upon each other and can, to a large extent, operate independently of the undergraduates. In our design the main pedestrian street is at the third level, at the edge of the hilltop. On that level and the two below it are the

44

Central meeting place

Administration (left) and Humanities wing (right)

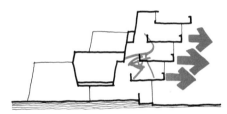

Diagram, outlook from the humanities wing

Interior, humanities wing

undergraduate facilities. On the two levels above are the graduate research facilities and faculty offices.

It was our decision that people should be segregated in their place of work when they needed privacy and a particular environment. But once they left that place to go somewhere else, for example to eat, they should use the same means of getting there as everyone else – the main pedestrian street.

Taking this down to detailed design created several anomalies. In one instance, the upper street of the Administration Building comes within 20 feet of the faculty restaurant in the Humanities Building. The shortest distance between two points is a straight line, and it would have been simple to put a bridge across the gap. But then the faculty and administrators on that level in the Administration Building could have gone to eat in that dining-room without becoming involved in what was happening in the rest of the College.

The original intention was to locate the major mechanical plant at the edge of the building. It seemed more sensible to put the plant at the centre, under the Administration Building. Hastie, the director of physical plant, hit the roof, pointing out that we would have to build a network of ramps and other expensive items to handle the underground traffic. But he relented.

The chimney design was an exercise in manners. We had two flues, but two chimneys looked rude. A fireplace was added to the faculty lounge to produce a third flue. There was no sense in emphasizing the matter then, but that fireplace has its own 60 foot chimney.

Construction

We worked at a furious rate. Using the critical path network as a guide, we started to dig holes for the hydraulic elevators before I was sure how many floors we would have; the footings were poured 10 per cent oversize because we had not had time to calculate the exact loadings. At times we were only hours ahead of the contractor, working madly to get

45

specifications out to him. The speed at which we moved was incredible, but it was the only way to meet the September 1964 deadline. On top of everything else we had to allow for the likelihood of a long construction strike in the summer. It happened and took five weeks to settle and we failed to meet the deadline. The University had to renovate an old building to accommodate the Scarborough students, and the cost was charged against the College costs.

Collaboration with the contractor was vital. The decision to use flying buttresses in the Science Building was an important example. The science laboratories were designed with the beams running 60 feet across them. These beams were not designed properly. The contractor had two floor levels up – still propped with forms – and was pouring the third when the engineer discovered that there was not enough width at the top of the beam to allow for buckling. There was panic at the site. We had our own panic at the office and reviewed possible solutions. I went out to the site. An obvious choice was to solve the problem locally by fattening the beam, but this would have completely altered the character of the building. I suggested a flying buttress connected to the top of the beam so that they would work together as a truss. I sketched the idea in the sand for the contractor and the engineer. They thought it reasonable. We went into the construction shack, drew up the specifications and the contractor went out and built it. That all happened within a few hours. The building looks five times better with the buttresses.

The concrete job is good, especially if the working conditions are taken into account. Given more time we could have refined the archaic formwork system. The site looked like the bridge of the River Kwai with thousands of sticks propping up the forms. During the winter we had to build a plastic house over the construction to enable the concrete to cure. It is hard to pretend that this was the most sophisticated way to build a building. The contractor had no more time than the rest of us to think about his problems in a leisurely manner.

The first concrete poured was turning a bright pink. Experts from Crown Zellerback discovered that the colour was the result of the reaction between the water in the concrete and the particular plastic coating on the plywood form. The plastic coating was changed but the pink concrete in that particular section is still there. No architect could hope to foresee these construction problems and handle them without the help of others.

As the contractor moved up from lift to lift spillage proved a problem. To cope with this we developed an economic method of formwork which also gave us the building finish. Form boards of any length were used, but at the top of the pour a triangle wedge was inserted. The wedge created the ledge for the next form and also acted as a plug against spillage. The result is that the matched walls are three-quarters of an inch thinner at each lift. Techniques such as this – for spillage, forming and wall ties – provided the decorative quality of the building finish, rather than preconceived ideas about visual aesthetics.

As soon as construction started, it became fashionable to predict disaster. The construction schedule was extremely difficult – half a million dollars per month and the contractor was having difficulties meeting it. The costs were high and the going became tough. If we had waivered, shown the slightest hesitation or loss of faith, the project would have been dropped.

The new Chairman of the Board did not have the same enthusiasm for the plan as his predecessor. The Chairman of the Building Committee informed us the University had decided to stop construction, cancel the project and start again. Anderson persuaded them to continue. Hastie was under tremendous pressure to turn against the project, but he refused to cave in. A firm of project management consultants were called in to investigate but they could find nothing wrong in the process of rectification. During this period we worked furiously to provide the contractor with working drawings to keep him

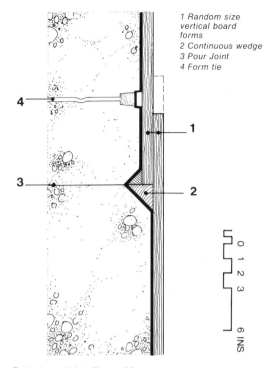

1 Random size vertical board forms
2 Continuous wedge
3 Pour Joint
4 Form tie

0 1 2 3 6 INS

Typical pour joint offset wall face

Detail of the science wing

going; a loss of momentum would have been fatal. The building was completed.

Comment

There are phases of a project within which fun and humour are appropriate, and then other phases when it is nuts and bolts and nerves more than anything else. Yet it was a good time and there were many occasions through Scarborough College when there was a party. It may have been at my place or it may have been at Bissell's, it was not as if we were the only ones reacting in a spontaneous manner. The whole Canadian scene was total involvement.

It was Beckel who described Scarborough College as a 'happening'. The combination of our talents, ambitions and frustrations, and the extreme conditions, forced us to the limit of our capabilities. There was no way to duplicate these unusual conditions – given a fractionally different mix, the entire effort could just as readily have ended in disaster.

There can never be another one; from then on everything had to become just that little more serious and responsible. In one way it was a completely irresponsible act, but it turned out to be a good building.

For a year after it was completed I hated to visit the College for I remembered only the details long considered and finally abandoned for reasons of cost or expediency; crude collisions in details, questionable finishes, nightmares generally. But those memories fade.

The greatest success of Scarborough College as a built form is its ability to allow the users to create their own community learning environment. For instance in our plan we had provided for a separate art gallery, with a separate entrance door. The College decided to use the original gallery area for offices and to relocate the art gallery out on the pedestrian street. As yet no paintings have been damaged or stolen, which seems to prove Jane Jacob's theory of surveillance. People no longer have to decide to move off their route and enter a separate room to look at art; it is there on the street creating a more natural, subtle relationship between artist and inhabitant. It is also a highly regarded gallery.

In designing the Meeting Place we had carried out acoustic tests to ensure that the reverberations from walking and talking noises were not excessive. No one thought then that the users would decide to use the Meeting Place for music and theatre performances which would be open to the public as well as to members of the College. Today it is an important part of the cultural facilities in the Metropolitan Toronto area, and particularly valuable to the residents of suburban Scarborough.

An architect, no matter how astute, cannot foresee these eventualities with accuracy. What he can and must do is create spaces which allow the users, within reason, to respond to changing demands of use. 'We make the space, you make the place.'

There are a number of complaints to be made about the plan and design. The first phase was designed for 1500 students, with the result that the first students, numbering about 500, were a little lonely and the spaces, including the Meeting Place, did not function as we thought they would. The steady increase in student population has helped to alleviate that problem.

The Science Building had so many good things in it originally that it was never subjected to the same intensive analysis as the Humanities Building. The result is that the Humanities Building is much better. The street in the Science Building does not have sufficient high-use destinations plugged into it to give it the pedestrian circulation it needs. We used lecture theatres to turn corners, with the result that the rooms have no natural light. The physical relationship between the faculty offices and laboratory facilities could have been better. The preparation rooms between laboratories are not used sufficiently because the college lacks the funds to pay staff to man them. The two lower streets are aptly nicknamed Belsen 1 and 2 – they are long, institutional-looking and generally dismal places to walk through.

The lack of natural light in the lecture theatres in the Humanities Building was due more to the political situation. The requirement was for theatres which could be blacked out. Our recommendation was for windows with shades or blinds. The janitocracy insisted that blinds or shades can be torn, someone has to look after them, and generally they are a nuisance. Quite simply, I lacked the confidence to make an issue out of it. Even at that stage I was winning battles more by chicanery and manoeuvring than by my face value as an architect. There were too many battles to fight and I let that one go. Probably, the windowless lecture theatres are the worst thing about the College.

I am not sure that the basic concept of separate Science and Humanities Buildings was the best one. The mixed use of the science laboratories was a pointer in the direction of a general mix of facilities. We could have, if we had looked at the requirements closely, created lecture theatres suitable for mixed use by science and humanities people. The existing division reflects a history of academic separation which should have no future.

The plan and design of Scarborough College derived from, I believe, a common sense synthesis to a number of extreme and conventional conditions. Consciously and deliberately we were reacting against the formalization and ritualization by others of the work of men such as Corbusier, Kahn and Aalto; men exploited by disciples who extracted from their work a vocabulary of form. It was our hope that Scarborough College would explain its own forms, that those looking at it would understand the attitudes that went into its design, the reasons why its forms are as they are. Instead, the forms have been formalized as a part of a 'contemporary style' in architecture and the reasons for them have been misunderstood or disregarded.

That is our greatest failure.

Kids and community

Andrews' stampede with the design and construction of Scarborough College initially had an adverse effect on his opportunities for further university commissions. An appointment to the newly instigated University Planning Office with Hough and Hugo-Brunt kept him engaged in planning rather than building. His interest in planning was simply as the preliminary to building, but buildings for the University did not eventuate.

Contacts made while building Scarborough College did, however, lead to the commission to build a small primary school for the nearby residential district of Bellmere. Bellmere School is a single-storey development following the organizational pattern of the Saulte Ste Marie Secondary School. Repetitive unit classrooms with pyramid roofs group around the main hall – the multi-purpose gymnasium. Domestic in scale, the building provides a comfortable sympathetic environment for its young inhabitants. It is a community building that blends visually and socially with its setting. Its potential for growth has been realized, as two additions employing the unit modules have satisfactorily extended the building without increasing its visual scale or detracting from its function. Bellmere School is an unpretentious solution to the needs of small children and the unpredictable demands of educational programs. The building is successful in meeting the general intent of its design, but is less satisfactorily resolved in detail.

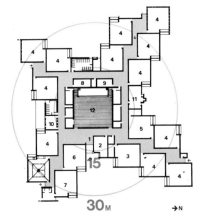

Circulation diagram, Bellmere Public School

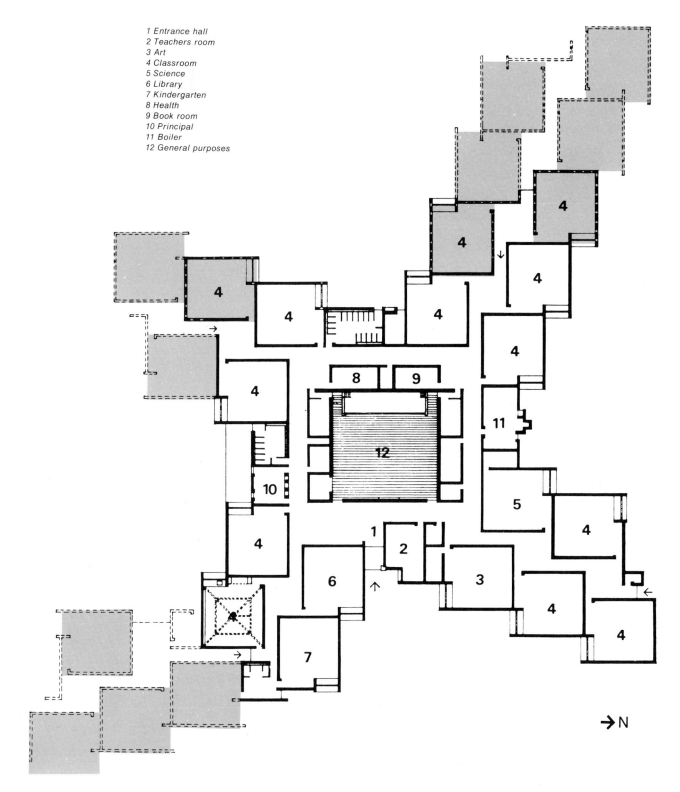

1 Entrance hall
2 Teachers room
3 Art
4 Classroom
5 Science
6 Library
7 Kindergarten
8 Health
9 Book room
10 Principal
11 Boiler
12 General purposes

→N

Proposed expansion diagram

Bellmere Primary School

During the development of Scarborough College we had had a number of meetings with officials from the Borough of Scarborough on various matters. The Chief Architect, of the Board of Education, Alex Taylor was a bloke that I knew. He was a friend of a friend or whatever. The Borough's director of education suggested I do a new public school that was in the offing. Scarborough College pushed Bellmere. The School Board at Scarborough really gave us the job because the College was being done and they thought we might as well try one of those. It was my first project without a senior partner or associate around my neck.

We had just moved into Colborne Street. The ground floor was taken and Dick Strong and I had the next one – I had a very small part of it. It was terribly important that we rent the two top floors. Along came an architect called Ron Thom who was moving from the west coast to Toronto. For some reason I cannot remember he would not go on the third floor unless I went with him. So in order to get someone in the place, I said okay. In the space of three months I was out the back with the elevator and the toilet and he had the whole front of the thing. Ed Galanyk during this time was still totally involved in building Scarborough College and that was when my second employee, Frank Final, joined me. There was also a student from Toronto who had ended up at the 'funny farm' for some reason. They allowed us to take him out if we gave him regular employment. The kid was okay – work commitment was the right therapy. There we were with Jim Sykes, a sort of ship's captain-carpenter-cum-architect, Frank Final, the kid from the funny farm, and me, all jammed into the one room with an elevator going up and down in our ears. It was a great place to produce a building.

The problem
The requirement was for a suburban primary school of some 11 classrooms, staff accommodation and a so-called general purpose room for assembly, sport and so on, with a stated need for the acceptance of growth how and when it became necessary.

So far as I could tell, the Scarborough Board of Education had built only standardized two-storey public school buildings with central-loaded corridors and a big bulge somewhere for a general-purpose room or gymnasium. The Board of Education actually supplied us with a book that set everything out including ceiling heights, room layouts and furniture specifications. It was obvious from looking at this book that school design in Scarborough was highly developed and that nobody had ever thought about it. You could have fed it all into a computer and ended with a building; the standardized two-storey formula based on vague economic considerations which did not stand up to analysis. Two storeys mean staircases, fire regulations and a standard of construction quite different and more costly than a one-storey building.

A two-storey building with a central loaded corridor could grow only at the ends of the corridor, in increments of four classrooms (or two if the second storey was not increased). It was impossible to expand the building in increments related more precisely to population growth, or in a form related integrally to the way the school might want to operate. The result was a long anonymous box with no identity as a school, or identity for the individuals within it.

The communities around these schools were simple, predominantly moderately priced, suburban, single-family homes with some small multiple units.

Suburbs may not be to everyone's taste, but people live in them and, presumably, they are happy to be there and want the place to be as pleasant as possible. In the midst of this is normally plonked a large institutional box with glass walls or punched windows which has nothing to do with its surroundings and not a lot more to do with education. It is not the sort of place a six-year-old can walk by with his mother or father and point out his room. The building is not fundamentally different in concept or design from the office building or factory his parents work in.

50

Classroom unit

The institutional atmosphere created by this type of approach infiltrates the school system itself. Educators take a child who has always lived in a domestic environment of a scale he has grown accustomed to and where he is surrounded by love and attention, and slam him into a great echoing box where he is treated like an enemy. The Board of Education had a tremendous number of preconceived ideas about children's behaviour. These arose out of the implicit conviction that, if not guarded and controlled, kids turn into savage, destructive animals. One of the very serious worries the administrators had about our design was that it was not possible to stand in one place and see the entire circulation system; you had to be able to do that because some eight-year-old might be bashing a six-year-old in a corner. Similar thinking to Scarborough College where only metal chairs were originally considered.

Bellmere brought me into conflict with the janitocracy. I am absolutely convinced that most public schools are not built for kids, they are built for janitors. That was the basic programming reference in the Board's book. A problem would come up. There would be a so-called solution in the book which suited everyone except the kids. Never would the reasons underlying the problem be examined. This procedure had gone on until it had reached the point where the schools were abysmal looking, inefficient and, worse still, rotten environments.

Our starting point was an environment having a lot to do with people from five to ten or twelve years' old. The Board was sceptical, especially about a one-storey concept, and we had to prove everything along the way – not a bad thing in itself.

The solution
The concept we developed was one of four clusters of one-storey classroom units grouped around a general-purpose area. Each corridor running off the corners of the central 'all purpose' room comes to a little space with two classrooms around that space, and then moves on to the next space. One cluster might

be for science and art students, another for the kindergarten, and so on. Using multi-comparison diagrams, based on statistics from other schools, we proved to the Board of Education that our one-storey concept had less circulation space than a two-storey building. A one-storey building avoided the inefficiencies and institutionalism of the central-loaded corridor structure and could utilize the concept of selected incremental growth.

It became possible in this way to add any number of units, one at a time if necessary, to any of the four clusters without disturbing what happened elsewhere in the school and without commiting the school to extensive, expensive alterations. We have in fact built two separate extension programs for the school.

The general purpose room is used as a gymnasium as well. Just as at Scarborough College we were told not to put in any windows. We asked why and were told the glare from the windows is bad for basketball players. We replied, 'That means no glare, not no windows'. Our solution was to allow the outside light to come in and wash down the two side walls, thereby avoiding glare and still providing a connection to the outside, and natural ventilation.

Outside the school we tried to keep a scale reminiscent of what a young person would remember from home. The classroom units look like houses, the roofs are peaks, the windows are house size, not great areas of plate glass, the little spaces outside the classrooms have skylights and are large enough for children to play in during wet weather.

Each classroom has a north-facing skylight and can be readily identified by the children as a particular place.

Comment
One of the signs of Bellmere's success was that some critics laid into us for not carrying the cluster concept further and developing a standardized module for a classroom unit which people could bang up wherever they liked. That criticism represents an approach to architecture typical of the work of the SEF. The SEF or Study of Education Facilities is jointly funded by the Educational Facilities Laboratories (New York) and the Ontario Government. There are years of hard thinking ahead of us to clear away the garbage which has accumulated into the so-called best wisdom about education, schools and building. Yet here are a lot of undoubtedly well-meaning, misguided people trying to translate misconceptions into standardized physical modules and make everybody use them. Standardization may have a place, but we are in no way ready for it. It is a poor excuse for clear, sustained thought about the problems involved.

Supposedly the economic arguments of SEF are unanswerable. Economies of scale are certainly considerable if you are manufacturing fifteen million identical light bulbs or wall units which everybody has to use.

I sometimes think architects favour SEF because they think it will help them cut building costs and keep the client happy. The constant complaint I hear from architects working with school boards is that the budget is too low for them to do the great work they would be capable of if more money were available. 'We cannot produce good design on such a low budget', they say. That is also absurd. School boards are reasonably realistic when it comes to setting a building budget. If the architect thinks it is too low he can always quit as a matter of principle. Or he can try to think the problem through, keeping within the cost limitations.

Bellmere came in $40 000 under budget when all the best advice we could get was that it would be $40 000 over budget, the building was different, the builder would be unused to the construction types, etc. etc. Coming back to the SEF argument, one of the reasons the building came in under budget was that all the components were standardized. They were the components any house builder had at his disposal and worked with every day. Bellmere was designed specifically for the small builder.

The school from the street

Rear view showing extensions

was, in that they had built small apartment buildings and stores. All these men could build in a way they were accustomed to without getting involved in a specialized building operation; the components were big timber purlins in the roof, cedar decking and standard shingles on top of that. It may not be important economically to the Borough of Scarborough or Manhattan to design schools which can be built by small contractors, but in innumerable small towns across the continent there are always one or two good house builders who could not handle a standard, two-storey school or factory, but could easily handle something like Bellmere. That would be important economically to those communities and provide reality to the popular talk about the integration of architecture and the life of the community.

Current school buildings required the services of a reasonably large contractor. Bellmere could be built, and it was, by a man who had never built anything in his life except houses. It probably could have been built by a couple of men down the street who were handy with tools.

Our small-house builder was not someone who wandered in from the cold and found himself with a building. It was a public tender. Only two bids on the first phase were above the budget. The successful bidder had trouble getting a bid bond because no one believed a non-institutional builder could build a school. He did not make much money on the job, but he by no means went broke and came back to tender on successive phases. The successful bidders on the second and third phases were also small builders; not unique, as the first was, in that they had built small apartment buildings and stores. All these men could build in a way they were accustomed to without getting involved in a specialized building operation; the components were big timber purlins in the roof, cedar decking and standard shingles on top of that. It may not be important economically to the Borough of Scarborough or Manhattan to design schools which can be built by small contractors, but in innumerable small towns across the continent there are always one or two good house builders who could not handle a standard, two-storey school or factory, but could easily handle something like Bellmere. That would be important

economically to those communities and provide reality to the popular talk about the integration of architecture and the life of the community.

The design was popular at the time and we had the dubious pleasure of seeing a very similar design win the Massey Medal for Architecture the next year. But basically, our school was crude in many ways. We did not develop the interior-cum-circulation spaces sufficiently in terms of the little people using them. There should have been more places to sit and more things conducive to play. We built and designed Bellmere with the same all-important attitudes that went into Scarborough College. The result was no less successful and its huge difference in scale began to crystallize my idea that all architectural problems are the same, they only vary in dimension.

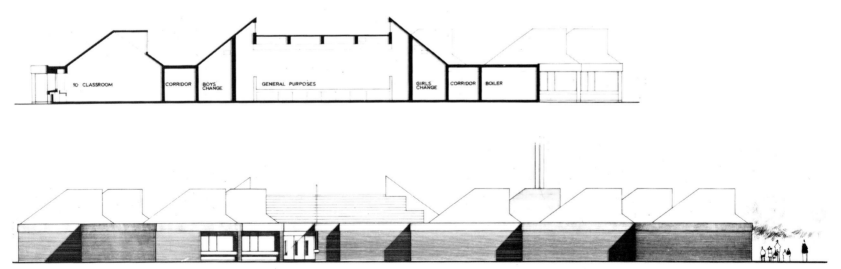

Section and street elevation

Shaping up
for social
concerns

Attuned with the mood of 1965 Andrews flirted seriously with the idea of multi-storied plug-in housing for itinerant workers. His scheme showed vertical frames supporting transportable standardized steel units, based in size on the largest available stamping presses – those used for box cars. This was an attempt at mass production according to the 'Henry Ford' principle. The purchasers would buy the desired number of connecting units. Variety was limited to such factors as colour and a range of attachable extras including balconies. Andrews continues to support the validity of such a vertical caravan stack to place workers near their places of employment and to conserve urban land.

The student dormitories for Guelph University, built in 1965, and Brock University, built in 1967 with Salter, Fleming and Secord, the associated architects, stand as testimonials to an attitude where the occupants' social needs take priority over strictly architectural determinants. The buildings are fundamental structures – economic enclosures for the life-style they were designed to accommodate. Both schemes consist of a piling up of small group clusters of individual sleeping accommodation, with shared bathing, living and limited cooking facilities, arranged along pedestrian streets and linked vertically by 'walk-up' circulation.

The University of Guelph required accommodation for 1760 students, as it was described at the time – 'a dorm city'. This was the first occasion in which Andrews faced the problem of providing an environment sympathetic to individual needs within the enormity of mass accommodation.

At Guelph the free form of Scarborough was replaced by a highly structured network based on a reversed pyramidal system of social grouping. The walk-up solution, arranged in a diamond grid around courtyards, dispersed the accommodation over a wide area of the site. The flat ground and the repetitive nature of the single-purpose use, provided little opportunity to relieve the visual impact of this extensive development. The number of students to be housed in the one complex was simply too high to admit any external semblance of domestic scale.

The internal planning intentionally allowed for freedom of choice, access and movement. However the assumptions made by Andrews regarding behaviour in such a situation have not been upheld. The common lounges, accessible by semi-public corridors to encourage use, have been stripped of their furniture and seating accommodation, and the private unit sitting areas, designed to permit a free flow of students, are rarely used. Guelph alone, of all Andrews' buildings, has been misused by its occupants. By contrast, the Brock dormitories, built two years later, which inhibit uninvited entry to the group living areas, function smoothly. While Guelph is an imposing complex, there is an artless simplicity to Brock's austere forms and finishes.

The pattern established in these two residences – low height, walk-up circulation, elevated streets, multiple points of entry, repetitive groupings of standard units or clusters, and close contact with the outside environment – persists in Andrews' work today where sites permit.

Axonometric of typical house arrangement

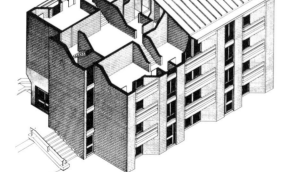

Brock University student residences

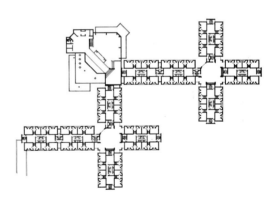

Typical bedroom floor

Student lounge

External court, Guelph University student residences

Guelph University student residence

Guelph University was created by an amalgamation of the Ontario Agricultural and Veterinary Colleges and the Macdonald Institute in 1964. The intention was to establish an arts and science college and instigate a balanced rapidly growing new university. The initial student population was 2300. The master plan was based on an enrolment of 6000 by 1970, 10 000 by 1975 and from 15 000 to 18 000 by 1980. The former colleges had existed for 100 years and had well established traditions.

Guelph was a small commercial rural city of about 40 000 people, with a predicted growth to 80 000 by 1980. There was little possibility that the city would be able to absorb a substantial proportion of students living off campus. Even in 1965 students were experiencing difficulty finding adequate off-campus housing.

The University had to plan and implement a large student housing program within an exceptionally short time. Originally we were approached by Evan Walker, the University's Housing Consultant, and a fellow Australian. He had completed a masters thesis at the University of Toronto on student housing and had subsequently been offered a contract by University of Toronto Press to publish a book on the topic. Initially we spoke about contractual procedures and other ways of meeting a tight time-limit. Subsequently we were retained for Housing Complex B, a project required to accommodate 1760 students.

The Problem

The client was well prepared. There was a master plan and a housing study, both of which presented their own problems but at least these were available.

The basic working document, and that which most influenced the design, was the study of student housing prepared by the Housing Consultant, Evan Walker. He had attempted to relate the University's philosophy and goals, and the nature of the student body to existing knowledge about student housing, and from this define a set of objectives and criteria for a housing program. These were based on stated

57

assumptions about the living and working activities of students, social interaction and group formation. At that time, this study represented a major advance in planning. Not all the recommendations held up under close analysis but the basic concepts enunciated by Walker were sustained.

The University had also created an organization to collect information and to make and implement decisions. The key figure was the Director of Physical Resources, David Scott. He was an engineer who knew how to use architects, who understood their problems and who was, unlike most engineers, sensitive to students. He saw them as individuals not as a mob of beings and was committed to creating a physical environment which they could use to meet their needs and preferences.

His thinking and operation reflected his clear understanding of the University's philosophy and goals, and his role in fulfilling each objective along the way. He let the architects do the work and retained for himself the final word. Once he was convinced of the proper course, he fought all the battles up through the University hierarchy to the Board of Governors and handled all the difficulties with the Provincial Government, particularly with

regard to financing. Occasionally the architects would go along to perform at a presentation but Scott bore the brunt of the politicking. It took some time for us to realize the full value of having him as a client. Working relations between us were not always harmonious but he had an interest in a common sense approach, was willing to listen and make and implement decisions and was an able organizer.

Quantity surveyors were retained by us to investigate the condition and capacity of the local building industry to handle a project of this size. Their findings were critical in the formulation of design criteria and the scheduling of the building program, for they ascertained that no contractor in the area was financially capable of handling a job of this extent if it was to be built solely of precast concrete or masonry or poured-in-place concrete. A strike in the masonry trade was forecast for 18 months hence.

As a result of this information the complex was designed to utilize basic building materials: poured-in-place concrete for the exterior structure and circulation system, masonry for the bedroom walls and precast concrete for the bedroom floors. The poured concrete was structurally independent of the other two

components. When the anticipated masonry strike became real the contractor continued pouring concrete. When the strike ended there was little left to do except complete the masonry work and the building in total was still on schedule with a changed emphasis in construction sequence.

The master plan called for high-rise accommodation. Keeping in mind the research carried out by the University's Housing Consultant we were convinced that stairs rather then elevators would provide the correct environment. For one thing, stairs are less expensive than elevators. More importantly, people would be more likely to communicate with each other as pedestrians on the stairs than they would while standing in elevators. If we were to meet the University's request for a socially viable and attractive environment we had to provide a solution which at least encouraged people to meet with each other. The opportunity to do so had to be there; it could not be created with an elevator system. No one believed 1760 students could be put on five acres with a walk-up solution. Our first problem, then, was to obtain approval to tackle this density on a low-rise basis and then solve it. The site presented another set of problems. By itself it was at first uninteresting, with no special features of topography, microclimate or

Student room

Basic unit is a room for each individual. The student can vary the furniture arrangement.

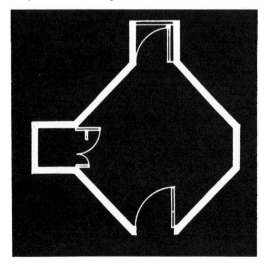

Six student rooms grouped around a landing and washroom facility, form a small social unit.

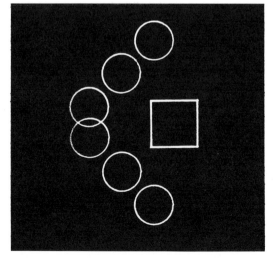

plant growth. It lay south of the main campus and the main University parking lots and was separated from them by a four lane road. At peak periods the road carried 1600 cars an hour to and from the parking lots and these peak periods coincided precisely with the periods of heaviest student movement from the proposed residence area to and from classes. We tried to persuade the master planners at the University to relocate the road but the master planners failed to be convinced. The University may have agreed with us but having spent a quarter of a million dollars with a particular firm and accepted their recommendations, no one was going to admit that a mistake had been made. The road stayed.

The University was concerned to create a community environment which encouraged students living off campus to mix with those living on campus. Because of the housing shortage in the city, the University estimated that ultimately 80 per cent of all students would live on campus. The dining and communal facilities in our requirements were to be designed to handle the extra 20 per cent. It was likely that students in residence would come to the dining-room for lunch although they probably would not want to go back to their rooms.

Therefore our recommendation was that the dining and major communal spaces be located on the north side of the road in the main campus area and that the study-bedroom spaces would be located as originally planned on the south side of the road. The road ran through a slight depression at this point and was deep enough to allow for the possibility of an elevated pedestrian walkway across it. In this way the two components would be connected, thereby avoiding any conflict between pedestrian and vehicular circulation.

The existence of an elevated pedestrian street over the road created the opportunity for developing a system of residences all of which were joined by an elevated pedestrian street to the main campus. By organizing this properly we could develop a situation similar to that at Scarborough College; a two or three-storey pedestrian environment within a six-storey volume. We had discovered already that this volume would handle the required number of students. No matter where they lived in the residence students would never have to walk down more than one and a half levels from the pedestrian street or more than three-and-a-half levels up. Any greater distance than that and elevators would have been necessary.

We had quite a go-around on that concept before the University agreed to this solution. The arguments against the concept were that it would foul up the master plan and eat up space which had been regarded as potentially academic in use. But there was an undeniable bloody logic to our concept. Nobody with a grain of common sense could dispute it. The concept was accepted.

The Solution
The critical element was the single room. The first group was to consist of not more than 16 persons, offering opportunities for both sociability and anonymity, grouped around lounge/kitchen/washroom facilities. The next grouping was the house, about 45 students, the number of persons a don could get to know reasonably well within a year. The house was to contain laundry and storage facilities. Five houses, or 225 students, five dons and a residence head would form a residence. This would be the most important social grouping. The group would be small enough for everyone to know everyone else at least on a nodding acquaintance basis. This group would constitute the basis for athletic teams, dramatic and theatre activities. The complex would consist of five residences related to centralized kitchen and eating facilities.

Each staircase system forms a house, with lounge and kitchenette for each group of twelve.

Houses grouped on pedestrian street form a residence, which has its own dining-room.

Preliminary architectural concept shows how actual configuration of rooms grows out of the diagram.

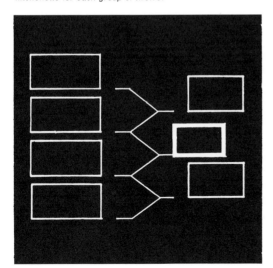
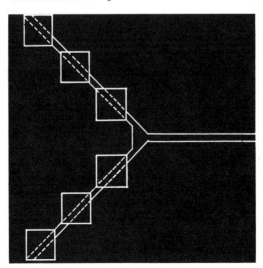
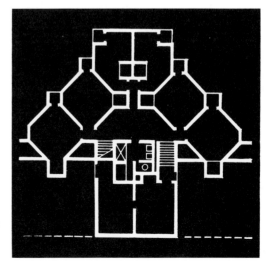

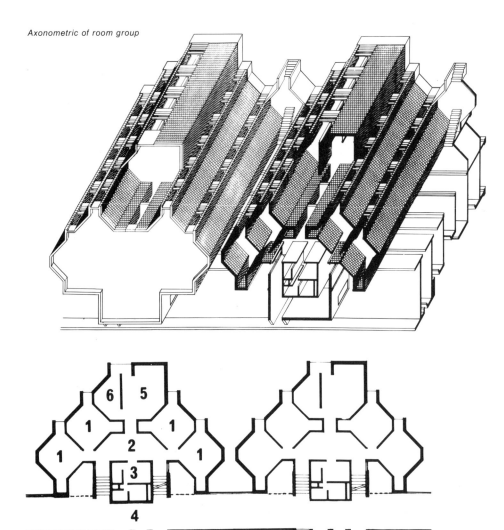

Axonometric of room group

Typical plan with grouped room units

1 Single room
2 Landing
3 Washroom
4 Pedestrian street
5 Double Room
6 Double study
7 Service

We began, as recommended, with the single room. The strongest design determinant was the University's requirement, based on Walker's recommendation, that we design a form of housing to accommodate movable furniture in the study-bedrooms. The purpose of this was to enable students to create their own environment as much as possible. At Morse College, Yale, the architect had tried to achieve this by designing hundreds of rooms, each slightly different from the other. The idea here seemed to be that this provided maximum diversity. This to my mind is nonsense because students and rooms were assigned. As soon as students are allocated rooms there is no freedom of choice. In the conventional room maximum flexibility is diminished because doors, cupboards and windows cut down the amount of wall space against which a student can put furniture, lamps, bookshelves. Our response was to develop a room in which all four walls were left free. The corners of the walls were chopped off and the doors and windows placed there. The window was a glass door leading to a tiny personal balcony. The furnishings and fixtures were then designed in proportion to the dimensions of the walls and of each other. This allowed the student at least 14 different major furniture-fixture combinations.

A small problem had to be overcome because the Federal Government's mortgaging agency, Central Mortgage and Housing Corporation, was prohibited from mortgaging chattels. Chattels include movable furniture, and without movable furniture we had no design concept and no way of meeting the University's basic social requirement. The University itself had no funds of its own. After a long battle the matter was resolved to everyone's satisfaction. When the Inspector from the Central Mortgage and Housing Corporation arrived to check the building and fixtures, the furniture in the rooms was fixed. After he left the butterfly nuts were unscrewed and the furniture became movable. Since then it has become legal for universities to finance chattels through debentures.

The room shape gave us a lot of soul-searching. The design was unusual and we had no way of telling what effect it would have on someone living in it. There was always the possibility that each Spring 1760 students would leave the residence suffering massive disorientation. We built a full-scale model of the room at the office and everyone took turns sleeping in it. We put a camera with a fish-eye lens in the ceiling and took pictures. We had a party in it and really tried to duplicate all of the ways it might be used. In fact we even did a couple of other things in it, but we did not get all that on film. A psychiatrist and psychologist were brought in, but our experience is that these people can tell you very little in a general way about the relationship between man and the details of his physical environment unless they have

done specific research. Finally we proceeded on the understanding we would use the room unless and until someone showed it to be harmful.

The basic geometry of the individual building or house was determined by two factors, the design of the room, and the need to provide each room with a reasonable share of sunlight.

Working with Walker, we lowered his original group size significantly. We decided that the first group would be a floor of six persons in four single rooms and one two-person suite. The six people would share a washroom. In a group of this size, there is the possibility of self-discipline and self-care. Anyone who does not flush a toilet or clean a sink will have the

others down on him; 16 people using a washroom are less likely to exercise the same degree of self-discipline. Also, six is not so small a number that a person wanting to be alone feels uncomfortable. Six is also the size of an average family, a unit that every student was at least familiar with.

The two-man suite in each six-man group consists of two unequal spaces within the area of the standard double room. The smaller space is large enough for one of the students to use for typing or studying if the other student is sleeping. We did not consider the standard double room, in which many inhabitants grow to hate each other, to be a desirable form of accommodation. But some were provided for those few students who preferred that option.

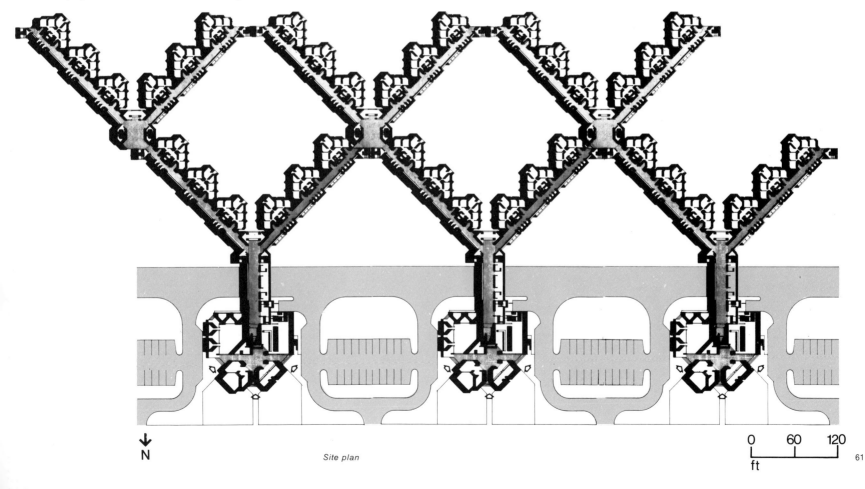

N

Site plan

0   60   120
ft

Each lounge area was planned to be shared by two groups of six, whose study-bedrooms were situated half a level above and half a level below. Rather than programming the lounge as a room with a door and sign which says 'lounge', this area was conceived as a wide space on the staircase landing with a sink, refrigerator and hotplate for coffee and snacks. This idea grew out of the University's concern to create a physical environment which offered students, mainly small-town and rural, who were not accustomed to living in this manner, ample opportunities to meet each other. They did not have to spend the rest of their lives together. But, if they were looking for someone to talk to they should be able to do so in a reasonably natural way. A lounge, therefore, was not something students had to make a conscious decision to enter. It was an integral part of the vertical circulation system of the building and would be used frequently.

If students did not feel welcome in their own lounge, they could always keep on going, pretending that they had something more important to do anyway, or there was someone in another lounge on the staircase they wanted to see.

Implicit in this concept is the theme of choice; the creation of a built-form which enhanced rather than discouraged choice. Although our thinking was often naive, at the time it represented a substantial advance on the interminable lines of double rooms marching along double-loaded corridors to community washrooms, being built in most other campuses across the country.

Five floors built around a vertical staircase constituted a house, with additional quarters for a don. The pedestrian street joined the houses into residences and the residences into a complex.

This physical arrangement does not differ remarkably from what you might find in an urban neighbourhood. The administrative system is supported by the organization of population by 'house'. The mail is delivered to each 'house', cleaning is picked up there, food and recreation are down the street.

It was important that the complex contain the most appropriate arrangement of spaces to accommodate changing social attitudes, as well as a population composition which was expected to vary widely over the years.

The forecasts as to population composition indicated that one sex would constitute the majority at the outset, but that over the years the imbalance would be reversed. There was no point in trying to be too specific about what was male or female accommodation, even though, theoretically, we could have built six separate buildings and satisfied the program.

At this time the Board of Governors was clearly concerned about women students away from home and what this meant in terms of physical accommodation which would facilitate separation of sexes and residence supervision. Even so, it would have been irresponsible to design a building which related primarily to this contemporary attitude. With advent of 'the pill' there was some possibility that women students would be able to look after

themselves reasonably well and that attitudes towards conventional segregation of the sexes in residence would alter. But the timing and content of these changes could not be predicted.

What was required was an arrangement of spaces which could be used by men or by women in varying proportions from year to year, while still allowing for whatever separation and control was felt to be necessary at the time.

Each of the five houses in a residence is physically separate from the other, although joined by the street. A house, therefore, could be all male or all female. Because of the location of the street, just above the midway level of the house, it would be possible to separate the top half of the house from the bottom half, one part for men, the other for women. The separation could also take place at the level of the washroom group.

We did not put urinals in the washrooms, only toilets, and a sanitary napkin dispenser which

Aerial view

Road overpasses between the residence and the main campus

can be covered with a screw-on plate. All options are open; thus the University has as much flexibility in the residences for segregation by sex as it cares to utilize. More important, perhaps, the University can, as some universities cannot, admit students of either sex without considering whether there is sufficient male or female accommodation available.

As far as possible, the major activities are located at the major intersections. There are two types of intersections or knuckles. Those joining streets to the bridge over the road are a point of information, a point of control, a place for joining and separating. This is where the porter is located along with the mail boxes, food and drink machines and other minimal amenities. The second type of knuckle joins residences together. It contains the same facilities as the main knuckles. Under the elevated street, at ground level, is an exercise room, not big enough for basketball, but large enough for informal games with mats and vaulting horses. The room has independent connections with each of the adjacent residences. Today the students hold dances on Saturday nights in the knuckles, but they will work much better on a day-to-day basis when the students can put more than the existing minimal social amenities in them.

Across the road there are three dining/ communal area complexes designed for the use of both students in residence and those off campus. Each complex can seat two hundred people at one sitting. The dining area itself is broken up into a large space with smaller rooms opening off it. This provides multi-use opportunities for a space which in most universities is empty for three-quarters of the day. The smaller rooms could be used for dinner meetings, or after meals for meetings of jazz groups, chess or whatever. The result is a much greater use of space per square foot than is usual in conventional dining areas. Each complex also contains a small library, a ping-pong room and several rooms for lounging, music and anything else the students might want to use them for.

Interiors of Guelph student residences

Hassles
Any design is worthless unless it can be built. At this time the Provincial Government was engaged in a public housing program for low-income families using the builder-developer method. The result was a remarkable increase in the amount of public housing produced, none of it particularly good. The Provincial Government decided to use the same approach for student housing, for Guelph was only one of the provincial universities in the process of rapid expansion and student housing was turning out to be expensive.

Guelph University listed its basic requirements (number of rooms, etc.) and Ontario Housing Corporation then called for tenders from developers who submitted proposals for an architectural solution and cost. The developer awarded the contract would be free to do very much what he wanted because the preliminary specifications offered no opportunity for control of the design. The developer's interest lay in building the project for as much below the tender price as possible in order to increase profit.

We received a call to go to Ottawa with the Ontario Housing Corporation to meet with Central Mortgage and Housing Corporation. Mortgage funds for student housing were provided by Central Mortgage and Housing Corporation, and Ontario Housing Corporation (later Ontario Student Housing Corporation) administered the program, handled the funds and provided the 10 per cent equity necessary to obtain a CMHC mortgage. The week before the meeting we worked hard to get as far into working drawings as possible. By the day of the meeting they were half-completed and it became clear at the meeting that but for this the scheme would have been cancelled and the project let out to tender on a builder proposal basis. Our instructions were to carry on with the concept and maintain the owner's objectives but lower our original price of $9250 per bed to $7777. No extra fee was provided; in fact OHC wanted to cut our fee although at the time our contract had been negotiated with Guelph University we had agreed on the minimum fee set by the Ontario Architects Association for complete professional services.

OHC thought that this minimum fee was too high. Also, they claimed that because of the repetitive nature of the complex, the fee for the second and third phases should be less. We argued that we had worked hard to achieve that repetition to afford savings in construction costs to the client and we were damned if we would be penalized for working in the client's interests. It would have been easy to design six different buildings.

We then received a letter from OHC demanding reduction of the fee. Our contract, however, was with Guelph University. OHC sent us a new contract. We refused to sign it until the question of fee was settled, claiming that our client was still Guelph until a new contract was negotiated. Scott stood by us and fought OHC. During the dispute we were revising the working drawings and preparing specifications although we were not sure we still had the job. The fight was not settled in our favour until the building went out to tender. Our victory over Ontario Housing Corporation, limited as it was, was pyrrhic. OHC officials refused to let us do any more public housing work. At a later date we prepared a proposal, in conjunction with a builder, for Lakehead University. The University selected our proposal; OHC absolutely refused to accept it. We were also asked by a major developer to enter into a joint venture for a major housing project in Scarborough. OHC told the developer he could use any architect he wanted, except us. That is the way it goes. Fortunately by the time this attitude had crystallized Brock Student Housing was well on the way.

The cut in costs for Guelph was achieved in part by juggling the financing arrangements and in part by stripping the complex to the bone. The general result was a deterioration of the quality of finish, not the concept. OHC was not overly sensitive to the physical requirements needed to create a decent environment, nor did it show much concern for students.

Faculty quarters were designated as double rooms and communal areas had double room put into them in order to get the bedroom

A dining hall

count up to a number which would give us bed count total cost ratio of $7777 per head.

In addition, we were able to persuade the Provincial Department of University Affairs that certain parts of the dining and communal areas should not be included in the cost of the residence because they served the University as a whole. The same was true for the service tunnels which had to be designed to carry University services as well as residence services. This turned out to be a game of passing numbers on pieces of paper back and forth among the various provincial and federal financing groups, each of which had to be persuaded to accept some of the costs.

Even with these cutbacks, we were having difficulty in getting the costs per bedroom down to the required level. In part this was because we did not make sufficient use of the quantity surveyors. We had already paid them for their earlier advice and, in effect, we had to pay them again for another job – a good argument for not relying on architects to retain a quantity surveyor out of their fees.

Because of the rush to get the project completed, the complex was to be bid in two phases, the residence first and then the dining-communal area. The bids on the residences were over budget. The lowest bid was $700 000 lower than other bids, but still $750 000 over budget. We then entered into discussions with the low bidder to reduce the residence costs still further. At the same time we worked with this bidder on the costing of the dining-communal areas. Then, we persuaded the University not to put these areas out for public tender, but to negotiate with the low bidder while everyone agreed to close their eyes. The University signed a two million dollar variation in the residence contract, with the same contractor to build the dining-communal areas.

Entry vestibule to dining hall

Cutting costs in the residence was as much an exercise in persuasion as in architecture. We reduced finishes as far as we could, but there were clearly limits to what could be done. The contractor had steel formwork left over from another project and offered to bring his price down $250 000 if this could be used instead of the plywood forms stipulated in the specifications. At that time we were not fully aware of the extent to which steel formwork is a design determinant. Steel formwork lacks the flexibility of plywood; it cannot be cut up with a saw as you go along, and that reduced our flexibility in problem solving during construction. However, without the steel formwork the complex might never have been built.

Our most difficult task was to persuade the contractor that he could make considerable savings because of the repetitive nature of the components. The repeated use of essentially simple components – precast concrete, masonry, poured concrete – would speed up construction by the workmen as they went along. The contractor, who for reasons of his own was determined to get this contract, decided to accept our reasoning and cut his price to the budget. The complex thus came in on budget, a budget imposed by OHC and unrelated either to the University's previously stated requirements or to the original solution.

1 Pedestrian street
2 Entrance vestibule
3 Meeting place
4 A dining hall
5 Dishwashing
6 To residence

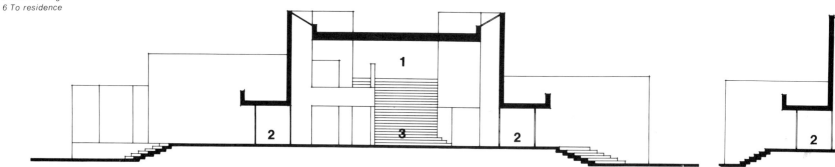
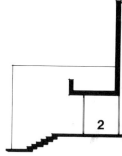

Cross section through a dining hall

In the early days of construction the situation appeared to be developing into a major disaster. Ned Baldwin, who had carried out all the negotiations with the contractor, estimated that at the existing rate of work the contractor would need five years to complete the complex. The quality of labour was poor and at first the contractor did not concentrate on efficiencies of operation. He did improve, however, and was able to achieve excellent savings in time and costs in the last stages, despite the predicted masonry strike.

There were three or four thousand doors in the project. Each had to be described thoroughly; what it was made of, its dimensions, finish, window type and size, hardware, location, time of installation. We wanted to develop a computer program for this but the $3000 for its implementation was unavailable. Fortunately the OHC insisted we extend our original schedule by one year and this enabled us to put another man on the job. He spent three full months detailing the door schedule. A computer would have taken three minutes.

Because of the special character of the rooms, we had been given the responsibility for designing and providing the furniture. We should have brought in an expert, but like most architects we thought we could design anything, especially something as ordinary as furniture, better than anyone else. We spent $10 000 and were delighted with our designs. A critic came from New York and pushed the designs down our throat. They just did not do the job.

After this experience we then brought in an industrial designer. His tenders were 40 per cent under budget, which meant we lost money with a fee on a cost percentage basis. (It hardly seems sensible to encourage an architect to keep costs down and then penalize him whenever he is successful.)

Another set-back occurred when a man in our office designed a lamp which, as well as being suitable for our particular needs, appeared to have enormous commercial potential. A prototype was built and royalty and other details were worked out. Then its designer, enthusiastic and eager to get things moving, rushed into the office late one day, shoved a work order for production of the lamp under the nose of one of the senior men who signed it without thinking too much about what he was doing. But the University had not yet approved the lamp and tests showed that the design to be faulty so approval was withheld. In the meantime the work order had been sent off and the firm making the parts in Holland had already started production and shipped off large numbers to the distributor in Canada. That came close to ruining us. The complexities of the legal entanglements are not worth listing.

So, after years of struggling to build a reputation and make a little money we were on the verge of being completely wiped out. At one point, potential lawsuits totalled $100 000. My practice, reputation and finances would have been destroyed. Eventually we got off paying only $7500 – the cost of the pieces built by the manufacturer to that date. The episode brought some painful lessons sharply home. Do not get involved in anything outside of architecture. Furniture designers design furniture, lamp designers design lamps, architects have to stick with what they do. It is hard enough to understand the limits within which you can even operate your own job. When other things have to be done, hire an expert.

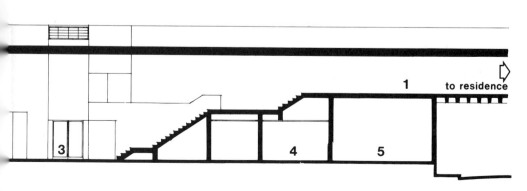

Longitudinal section through a dining hall with bridge to the residences

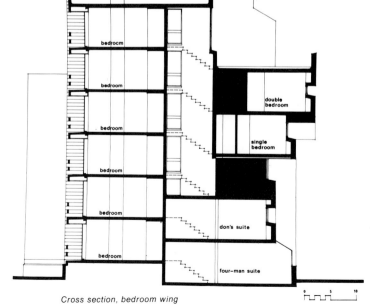

Cross section, bedroom wing

Our problem had become communication within the firm. From the beginning we had operated as a small highly integrated like-minded group of intelligent and capable architects who worked closely together. The myth continued long after it ceased to be true. We had a great deal of work and there were 25 or 30 architects in the office. Although the firm was successful and had an excellent reputation it was beginning to come just slightly apart. We were very vulnerable and lucky to be hit by only the lamp incident. It was essential to take hold, and set up lines of communication, allocate responsibilities more clearly and to define roles. Management consultants were brought in to look at our operations. Their final report was useless, but their presence made all the staff realize the importance of good management, careful decisions and good communication.

Approach to dining hall from the main campus

Comment

A year after Housing Complex B first phase was completed the students asked me down to talk about the project. It was interesting to find they understood what it was about. For the first six months the place had been awful. Students had thrown all sorts of garbage from their balcony into the courtyards, there was mud all over the carpets and cigarettes butted in the furniture. But once the students settled in the threat of a new environment had disappeared and such incidents did not occur again.

The reaction of the janitocracy was interesting. During the planning and design stages they had nothing favourable to say, but once the building was up and they moved in they were delighted. The chief janitor had the good grace to call up to apologise and say he had been wrong. The janitors had been most concerned,

Internal stairwell

for example, about the problem of keeping the boys out of the girls' rooms. They felt the balcony window doors in the ground level rooms presented an invitation for the boys to cross the courtyard, jump over the balcony, nip into the room and rape a girl or two. No such thing happened. Apparently such gymnastics were unnecessary.

As a piece of construction Housing Complex B is sloppy. This is partly due to the consequences of using steel formwork in a job detailed for plywood forms. It is also partly due to poor workmanship; men proud of their work would have done a better job.

Although Complex B has been described as the best student residence in Canada if not North America it is by no means a definitive answer. Some of the concepts are crude and not thought through properly. However it seems to be working. Six is still an arbitrary number for a washroom grouping. The circulation system allows the individual ample opportunity to make choices about those with whom he will associate but within the six-man grouping itself more might have been done to create options.

We would have preferred not to do another student housing project until we had seen how Guelph worked. However, a friend asked us to associate with him on a housing project at Brock University. We re-used all the main components from Complex B: the separate dining/communal facilities; the walk-up environment; the enclosed pedestrian street; the house system and the six-man grouping. Hopefully we refined and improved them. In these residences each group was provided with a lounge and washroom in the manner of an apartment rather than a dormitory. The street became a long student centre, a continuing sequence of entrances to houses, student offices, meeting rooms, billiard rooms, television rooms, and laundry. Food and drink machines were situated there. It should also have contained a short-order food place, but strange as it may seem in the continent of the hamburger joint the only place students can eat is in the dining hall.

Then everything happened

Everything happened at once in 1967. The Andrews family – and he now had four sons – had moved to an old house at Elora, 75 miles north-west of Toronto. The position as Professor and Chairman of the Department of Architecture at the University of Toronto enabled Andrews to design his own problem-oriented teaching program. At the same time the pressures of private practice escalated. The appointment of Peter Prangnell as an additional professor, to initiate and steer the revised curriculum, was a stated condition in Andrews' acceptance of the post. The new teaching structure aimed at an integrated framework that evolved around, and was closely tied to, the set design problems. This upturned the status quo and generated many enemies.

Andrews' time in this role at the University was short, but the importance of his influence on the new program has been clearly expressed by Prangnell, the next chairman.

'(Those) who have made the Toronto program what it is . . . have given me the most remarkable eight years of my life.

To be precise, I owe the years to John Andrews. As Chairman of the department he brought me to Toronto and gave me the opportunity to work out a programme which, after one year's trial, was adopted for the whole five-year Bachelor of Architecture course. Without John's perception and support, we wouldn't be discussing the Toronto program, because it would not exist. One of the most successful practicing architects in Canada, John paradoxically gave unqualified support to an academic program which was, in those early years, criticized savagely for its non-vocational approach. A further paradox is that the first model for this anti-establishment program in those formative years was the professional office, or to be more specific, John Andrews's own office in Colborne Street.'

Involvement in construction for Expo '67 at Montreal, selection as architect for the new sea terminal at Miami, the commissions for teaching facilities for Sarah Lawrence College, Bronxville, New York, for Weldon Library at London, Ontario, and for the Metro Centre project for Toronto, all occurred at approximately the same time.

Work in Progress, The Department of Architecture, University of Toronto, 1973–75.

During 1967, the students of the University of Toronto were given the opportunity to select their own designer for the new student centre – they chose Andrews. The problem of too much building on a totally inadequate site was not satisfactorily resolved. The University master plan was a point of contention, and further analysis suggested that dispersed facilities through the campus rather than a centralized core structure would better service student needs. A later study undertaken by the students themselves reached similar conclusions. The project became a 'political football' and, perhaps fortunately, the scheme was abandoned.

Preliminary design (1965) for Expo '67 included Commonwealth Place, a shared pavilion for participating Commonwealth countries who did not have the desire or financial resources to invest in an independent structure; African Place, for African nations with similar inclinations; and Activity Area F, one of several scattered relaxation and refreshment zones provided for in the master plan. Both Commonwealth Place (of fibreglass units) and African Place (of plywood sandwich panels) were designed as groupings of single-cell pavilions that could expand and contract depending on the demands for space. Lack of interest by the small Commonwealth nations resulted in the disbanding of Commonwealth Place, but African Place survived.

The masonry construction of African Place has considerable precedence, but the panel system gives a rare consistency to the concept. Financial limitations, and possible changes in requirements resulted in an adaptable, temporary, inexpensive solution that utilized the free benefits of the environment – terrain, wind, space and sun. Though far from satisfactory in its final internal arrangement, the repetition of the flexible basic spatial unit provided, as with Bellmere, an economical solution to an indeterminant program.

Model, Commonwealth Place Expo '67, Montreal

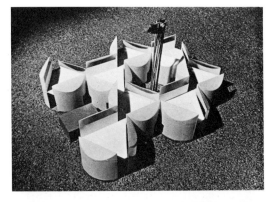

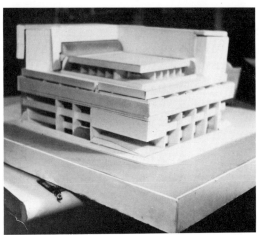

Model, student centre, University of Toronto

African Place Expo '67

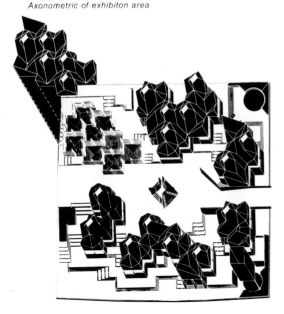

Axonometric of exhibiton area

Nobody at the upper levels of power asked us to do a job at Expo '67. We knew a fellow working there who was in a position to know what projects could possibly happen, and he literally manufactured a thing called African Place. It started out as a little pavilion.

The Canadian Corporation for the World Exhibition 1967 had set a minimum limit of 3000 square feet for pavilions to prevent people from building closets and calling them pavilions. The limitation clearly excluded a number of poor countries from participation in the fair. CCWE realized that if it wished to achieve its aim to register more countries than any other previous world exhibition, inexpensive rental facilities would have to be provided.

The emerging African nations did not have the money to build a grand pavilion nor the money to demolish it after six month's occupation so the Canadian Government decided to build a complex in which they could all have a little piece – even 300 square feet.

The result was African Place. Originally it was intended only for African members of the Commonwealth but the restriction was lowered and many French-speaking African countries applied for space. A capacity for growth and change was essential, for emerging African nations were continually changing their mind about participating and about the amount of space they required. The pavilion was more successful than expected and about two dozen countries eventually took space. New countries kept signing up, while others failed to put up the money; this resulted in changing and rearranging the pavilion even while it was under construction.

The successful construction of African Place, and of Expo '67 as a whole, was the work of one man, Colonel Edward Churchill. Despite a widespread belief that it could not be done at all, and certainly not on time, he built the islands for the sites of all the structures. He used critical path extensively; without it he would probably not have succeeded. Much of the time I thought he was a tough bastard, but

he was a decision-maker and it was plain that he knew his job and intended to do it. He was fair, willing to let the architect play around until the critical path schedule said that time was up. Then Churchill went ahead and built what was on paper, regardless of how it looked. Once you accepted that the rules of the game provided no divine rights for architects it was simple to work in that environment.

The problem

The first problem was to register in Quebec. As I was not a Canadian citizen I could not register. A senior Quebec architect was approached with the offer of a joint venture and he offered in return to stamp anything we did for a flat 20 per cent of the fee! However about this time, Bob Anderson, who had taken out citizenship papers, joined the firm and was able to register in Quebec. I associated with him and thus the job was kept within the firm. This discrimination is widespread. Mies van der Rohe designed the Toronto-Dominion Centre, but nowhere can you find his name on it.

We also had to establish an office in Montreal as part of the prerequisite, so we rented a one bedroom apartment and Frank Final spent some of the time down there.

We hired a French architect (actually Algerian French) because all the drawings and specifications had to be in English and French. By that time we had African Place and 'Area F', a facilities area of shops, restaurants, some toilets and heaven knows what. The work amounted to three or four million dollars. It was not a great deal but it was enough. Canada was booming at that time. Everybody had work.

The sleeper train left Toronto at 11.59 p.m., arrived at Montreal at 8 a.m. and for about a year or 18 months we were constantly catching that train. I have jumped on the train almost as it was moving, carrying drawings still wet with ink. We would get on the train, have a few drinks in the bar, go to bed, get up in the morning, get off the train, go to the apartment, have a shower, eat (there was a Hungarian restaurant around the corner which really had good breakfasts), then go to Expo. They had a multi-storey office building for headquarters. And you knew bloody well, there was no question, you had to take them out to lunch and that was it. Out to' lunch you would go, then there would be a series of meetings. You would try to avoid taking them out for dinner because it was right at the time when discos were starting in North America and there were a couple of really good ones in Montreal. So we would go to a disco, have dinner, go to another disco, get poured onto the 11.59 p.m. train, back in Toronto at 8 o'clock in the morning, then the train to the office and back into it all again.

I do not know how we stood it. In architecture you cannot work and pace yourself so that every day is a nice ordered sort of a day. Everything always finishes up in a hell of a rush.

For example, at 11.59 one night I was leaving for the final presentation on African Place and the model was not finished. The presentation was the next morning at 10 o'clock. I got on the train with just the drawings. John Simpson and Frank Carter were left in Toronto working on the model. They rented a station wagon, left Toronto at 5.30 in the morning to get to Montreal at 10'clock and it is a five hour drive! As I heard later they got in that wagon and roared down the 401 to Montreal. At Kingston they were doing better than 100 miles per hour and noticed a police patrol car behind them. Frank was driving so he slowed down a bit and the police car went off on the slip road into Kingston, so they thought. So Frank put his foot down again and they got up over the ton but unknown to them the police car came down the other slip and pulled behind them again and stopped them. They got a speeding ticket for something like 40 dollars. They got there exactly on time and we somehow managed to slip the speeding bill in to Expo and they paid it. But there I was sitting at the other end, and I knew none of this. I was on at 10 o'clock and at 5 to 10 they were not there with the major piece of presentation, but at

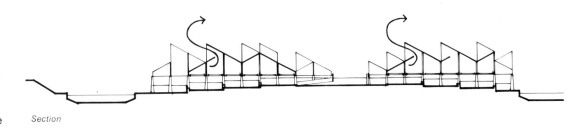

Section

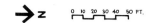

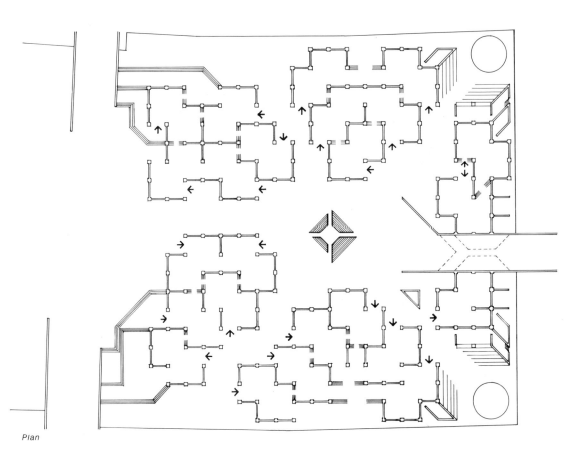

Plan

about half a minute past 10 in came two haggard-looking individuals. It has always been like that but we have never missed.

The site was a small knoll by the edge of the St Lawrence River with man-made canals on two sides. Our task was to design a series of spaces (on a total budget of approximately $1.2 million) to accommodate African countries wishing to rent exhibition space. Montreal is hot in the summer but clearly there was no money for air-conditioning. Even if the money had been available, it would have been impossible to design an air-conditioning system for something constantly growing and changing, no one knew how many exhibitors there would be or how much space each would want. The building had to be designed so that as much of it as possible could be manufactured off the site and brought to the site for easy assembly, with thought given to disassembly and re-use elsewhere. Obviously the design had to be simple. With the massive amount of construction taking place at Expo, the construction industry was inundated with work, so we had to design something to attract small builders who were unable to handle the larger Expo projects. As it was, we received only two bids for African Place. With anything more complicated, we might have had no bids at all.

The solution
The solution was a conglomerate of 300 square foot spaces changing levels within the levels of the site. An open-wall system enabled the pedestrian to see from one level to another, constantly referring back to where he had been and forward to where he might want to go.

The structures enclosing the spaces were one-storey frame plywood trusses supported on terracotta tile walls and piers. It was possible to add or subtract from the number of units depending upon the need; limits were imposed only by the ultimate site area. An exhibitor could rent a cluster of spaces as one large space or have as little as 300 square feet.

Environmental control we tackled by using

wind. The meteorological survey showed a steady prevailing wind across the site from the river during summer. Each structure was designed with a reverse wind scoop; that is the scoops faced away from the wind. This created a venturi effect around the scoops, drawing out the hot air from inside the pavilion and thereby creating a natural air-conditioning system.

The visual similarity with Bellmere is apparent. In each case we needed to handle a program which was defined but open-ended, to accommodate growth and change, to create an immediate sense of atmosphere, and to handle circulation. But the results are quite different.

Comment
African Place is one of the purest responses I have made to a problem. It met all the requirements including that of the budget. We were three per cent over the estimate; the next lowest building was something like 50 per cent over budget and some were eight times budgeted costs. The only other building which originally met the requirements of off-site manufacture and possible re-use elsewhere was Buckminster Fuller's geodesic dome for the United States Pavilion. Here a decision was made to weld the components together instead of bolting them as originally stipulated; for all practical purposes even the dome is permanent.

The major failing of African Place is the interior. We had hoped to co-ordinate all interior designs but the contract was awarded to a Paris firm which was totally unsympathetic to the basic concept. The exhibits were designed and manufactured in France without any significant reference to the structure. The designers took the ceiling heights as constant and treated each space as a box with no windows, set up exhibits in standard display cases and stuffed them in. The result was catastrophic. Walls were filled in so that tourists could not see or move from level to level thereby destroying the basis of the movement system and any incentive for exploration. Each space has a triangulated roof for the wind scoop. The original intention

was to use these overhead spaces to hang displays from, or project displays into. The designers put in ceilings which cut off an entire dimension of space and perspective and ruined the natural air-conditioning system. We fought a running battle with the designers and lost every round. Such is the separatist problem. It was very real even in 1967 – it was France versus England.

Nonetheless, the response to African Place was extraordinary. The most frequent comment was that we had set out to create a contemporary version of an African Village. In fact, we had started with no preconceptions of what the structures might look like. The design arose completely and simply from a response to the client's requirements, site conditions and the needs of exhibition space. Thinking about it, one can see that an African Village has to meet many of these same conditions; a conglomerate of spaces capable of growth and change to meet unpredicted needs, inexpensive, using readily available material which can be easily assembled by anybody and taken down and reassembled some place else, and there is even the ever present need for natural air-conditioning. African Place illustrates perhaps as clearly as any project how similar problems lead to similar solutions when the concern is to respond in a sensible, common sense way.

Precedent
for passengers

For the Miami Passenger Terminal a similar approach to climatic conditions, circulation, and the repetition of basic units gave rise to a markedly different physical solution. The Miami Port Authority called for a structure that not only accommodated an efficient system for the passage of travellers and goods, but for a building that would serve symbolically as the gateway to Miami. A previous scheme by the consulting engineers had been rejected on the recommendation of Professor Giurgola of Columbia University, who acted as advisor to the Authority. The rejected scheme had many failings, among these being the lack of compatibility of the rather mundane solution with the festivity of holiday arrivals and departures.

Andrews was selected from three architectural firms recommended as suitable to work in collaboration with the engineers in the preparation of a new design. Patterns of movement of people, luggage, goods, vehicles and ships provided the basic rationale for the scheme, which developed as a linear multi-level structure interrupted along its length by nodal points containing passenger lounges and related facilities. The efficient flow system replaced the usual chaotic scene typical of most shipping berths. Open corridors and the orientation of the building to the waterfront scene of the comings and goings of vessels involves the passenger in the activity of the port as soon as the building is entered. The dramatic curving roof with the aerofoil shape was derived from wind-tunnel tests on what was basically an open shelter in a hurricane area. An extra bonus was gained from the visual possibilities of such a form to reinforce the sense of movement.

The imagery of Miami arises from its response to the extreme natural forces of its location, and the delineation of the activities within. There is no precedent for this building amongst the shipping berths of the world.

Vehicular approach to
the terminal

Miami Port Passenger Terminal

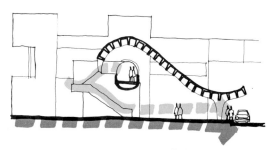

Aerofoil roof, Miami Passenger Terminal

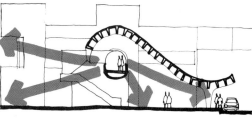

Pedestrian circulation

Visual connections

Light and air

We were invited to meet with the Port of Miami Authority to discuss a new port terminal. It was necessary to fly to Miami. I hate flying and used to drink my way through flights. By the time we arrived for the interview I was in a state, having had a bad flight and some suspect shrimp for lunch. Standing there in the Port Authority's pseudo-Jacobean boardroom, I suddenly felt queasy. I put my hand over my mouth in time, bolted for the bathroom, came back and finished the presentation. When you go into a presentation you have to have some means of being remembered.

I was quite aware that the other two architects on the short list were noted for their design capability. We emphasized the organization of our firm and its ability to produce a building on time within the budget, using critical path method and cost control; while letting good design – so-called – be a by-product. This approach, carefully thought out, was to me the obvious performance necessary to get the job, and this time I was right. If nothing else, Scarborough College and Housing Complex B, Guelph had taught us that good designs sitting in sketchbooks are worthless unless they can be built.

We were brought into an architectural can of worms. An engineering firm had been working on the project for some time with no success. Its design for the terminal had been presented to, and rejected by, the Port Authority which then insisted that architects be called in. In fact the engineering firm had completed a full set of working drawings.

Three per cent of the project cost was allocated for fees. We agreed to do the design itself for two per cent, and let the engineering firm produce the working drawings and supervision for the remaining one per cent. In addition, we obtained a $10 000 fee for preparing the master plan for the project, and a lump sum to cover the costs of providing a project architect in Miami during working drawings and periodic site visits.

When we were in the first stages of Miami a prerequisite was that we build a model. To make any sense it had to be pretty big and it ended up about eight feet long. Jim Sykes prefabricated the model in Toronto and the nicely cut out bits of wood were transported in a box to Miami where we had use of the Port Authority's workshop with all the machinery in it to put it all together. That was another presentation I had to start without a model. Half an hour late in came these architects who had been working on the model, looking like navvies. Jim Sykes, still in a blue singlet covered in sawdust, proudly carried the model into the boardroom of the Dade County Port Authority.

Our client was the engineering firm. This was potentially unsatisfactory because we had no legal relationship with the Port Authority and in particular with its director, Admiral Stevens. But we established a strong, albeit informal, relationship with them which was sufficient for the communication we needed.

Construction had begun on a new harbour port in the middle of Biscayne Bay on a man-made

island of crushed coral. The sea-wall was already built. The solution for the terminal would have to take a linear form.

Ed Galanyk, Ned Baldwin and Ian Morton were sent to Miami for a three-day cruise to experience the process of embarkation, shipboard living and disembarkation. The three were unanimously and solidly negative in their reaction to the disembarkation process.

When a ship tied up in port the motors were turned off with the result that the air-conditioning could not function. The law forbids the serving of drinks on US ships tied up in US ports, as they are inside the three-mile limit. The baggage was taken off and sorted before the passengers were allowed to disembark for customs. The entire process consumed about five hours. There the passengers sat, after a happy, romantic voyage, sweltering in the Florida heat without anything to drink, and then fighting to find their bags, pushing and shoving through customs for five miserable, hot, irritating hours.

One of the conditions was that we had to work in Miami. We worked in the Admiral's boardroom right next to his office. There was Ian Morton, Ed Galanyk and myself. Ned Baldwin and Dick Strong also spent some time down there. In a situation like that, when you are awake, you work; work like hell all the time.

We had a constant supply of beer and it got to a point where, when the Admiral came in (he would drop in 10 times a day), he had to push the door open and push the beer cans out of the way. That room was just left – it was not cleaned for a month. The job was done, designed and everything else but you should have seen the room. That is still one of the major stories down there – 'When the architects were designing that building you should have seen the beer they drank'.

The problem
The problem was to design and build a $4.5 million passenger terminal for the 'Sea-Gypsies' – tourist ships plying between Miami and Nassau, Jamaica and elsewhere in the

Location of passenger terminal in the harbour port of Miami

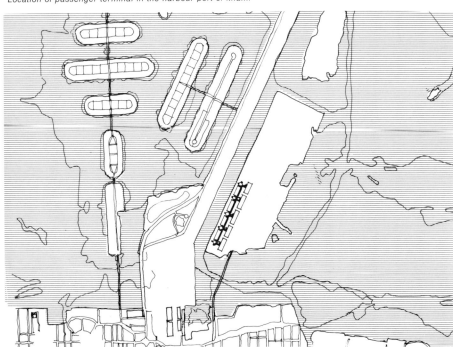

Aerial view

Caribbean for three, four, five days at a time, continuously throughout the year.

It became immediately obvious that disembarkation was the critical problem to be solved if cruising was to retain its euphoria after the cruise.

The two previous designs by the engineers had reflected an attempt to handle five ships almost simultaneously in one big collection area. We discovered, however, because of the narrowness of the channel and the subsequent need for pilots, that the ships could only dock at 30-minute intervals.

If the customs and immigration operation could be revamped and split up to handle ships individually, the nature of the problem would be altered and partially resolved. There did not have to be one large collection system to handle all the ships at once; there could be separate collection points.

The solution

The solution is based on five separate points or nodes of embarkation and disembarkation. These nodes are lounge-type spaces connected to the ship, but situated on land. In this location they could be air-conditioned by a land-based system and refreshments could be served. Contact was available by telephone and waiting friends could be recognized.

Customs and immigration agreed to divide their staff into teams to handle the ships as they come in. Each ship has three decks and a fore and aft. Any passenger can remember his deck number and whether his cabin is fore or aft, especially if he has a ticket with this information. On board he tickets his baggage and keeps the stub. The ship's baggage is now in six small packages instead of one large one.

The passenger walks off the ship into the aerial lounge where he waits in comfort until

his baggage is ready. The baggage is off-loaded and put in order in the customs area according to deck and cabin position.

The lounges or nodes are connected to each other by a long tube covered with an aerofoil hurricane-resistant roof. Between each pair of lounges are six sets of stairs to the customs and immigration area. Each stair corresponds to a deck number and cabin position, fore or aft. When the baggage is ready the passenger, clutching his ticket stub, walks along to the proper staircase, descends, finds his baggage, clears customs and leaves. We were able to devise a system to clear passengers within 45

Diagram of ship tie up sequence and baggage distribution

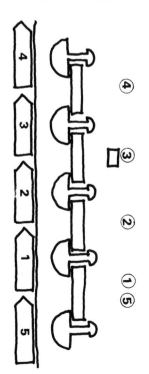

Shipside passageway

to 50 minutes of docking instead of the usual five hours. In fact passengers are being cleared in a maximum of 40 minutes.

It is instructive to compare the environmental analysis used for the Miami terminal with that used for the Toronto International Terminal (or most other airport terminals). For Miami, we tried to create a human environment in keeping with the activities and atmosphere related to sea travel, and to organize baggage handling, customs and immigration in a way that would sustain the environment. At Toronto International Airport, the baggage is handled beautifully and conveniently, straight off the plane and into the baggage carousels. But the people on international flights are trudging up and down long, dismal lavatory-like corridors, through vast stockyard corrals, and queuing up like a herd of poor, bloody cattle. The principle here seems to be that it costs money to move baggage but people can move themselves. If architects are concerned about people, their concern should be to move the people as directly and comfortably as practical and find some machine to cart the baggage the long way around, if that is the choice.

In a technological society architects have shown a mediocre competence in organizing the pieces of technology, for example moving baggage cheaply and quickly from point A to point B. In the midst of these mechanical arrangements, the people are left to wander for themselves. The grave and possibly fatal weakness of contemporary architecture is that it has so far failed to utilize the capabilities of technology to accommodate man as well as baggage.

Our solution provided a number of side benefits. We could build the terminal progressively, with each module fully operational as soon as it opened. Because the clearance time was cut to about one-eighth, customs and immigration could operate more efficiently. The first ship would be almost cleared by the time the second arrived, and by the time the fifth ship arrived, the first three would be cleared and the fourth would almost be completed.

The terminal from the water

Originally, the tubes were to be covered with a
curved glass ceiling under the aerofoil roof, so
that they could be air-conditioned along with
the lounges. The pre-bid estimates from the
major glass companies were about ten dollars
a square foot for the curved glass, which
suited our costing at the time. But when the
tenders went out, each of the glass companies
bid about $45 a square foot. That meant almost
a million dollars – one-fifth of the total budget.
We took the glass out and restricted the air-
conditioning to the lounges. The glass
companies then offered to produce the glass
for a lower price; they might even have come
down to ten dollars again. We told them to
forget it. I had no use for that kind of trickery.
In any case, other parts of the building were
more expensive than expected, so it suited us
to eliminate the curved glass completely.

Comment
The organization of functions does not mean
what is currently understood as Bauhaus
functionalism: the shortest distance to the
toilet. Function is as much a matter of
environment as it is of distance and
measurable convenience. Functionalism must
relate to people in a common sense way, not
through ritualized formulae.

Basically the building is designed to transfer
people from one mode of transportation to
another. Possibly not enough attention was
paid to developing the in between spaces
where passengers could say goodbye to
friends and greet them on returning. But the
building was cheap: half a mile of structure for
only $4.5 million.

The Port Authority is delighted. The number of
ships using the terminal tripled even before
the first five nodes were constructed. The
master plan calls for five nodes in the first half
mile; then expansion by turning a corner.
Fortunately the island site will prevent the
terminal from being recreated *ad infinitum.*

In its way the terminal is the perfect job. The
solution is straightforward, reflecting what was
in essence a simple problem of transportation.
Transportation structures are our
contemporary cathedrals.

Circulation is . . .

Weldon Library, University of Western Ontario, London, was designed in association with the local architectural firm of Murphey and Schuller. This Library broke with that University's tradition of stone structures, which by the 1960s were appearing in a debased form of veneered contemporary construction. It is the last of the buildings designed by Andrews' firm that has close structural and organizational affinities to Scarborough College. Many of Scarborough College's solutions to problems of detailing and articulation appear again here. Yet the studied resolution of structure and the immaculate finishes of the Library's finely corrugated concrete wall-bearing construction provide a marked contrast to the earlier building.

The opportunity was taken to utilize the building to join the pedestrian paths of the campus. This necessitated the use of two entrances and two check-points. The central double-height entry hall is overlooked by a mezzanine, and lit from above around the edges of the waffle slab ceiling. The work areas fan out from these circulation spaces. Connecting bridges add to the complex spatial interplay.

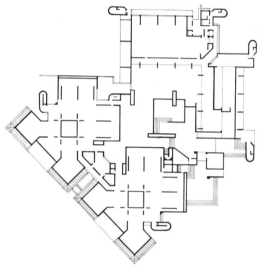

First floor plan, Weldon Library

Though small in size, the structure and organization of Andrews' office was such that it could undertake the management and construction of urban-scale projects. Bob Anderson joined the firm in 1965 and the office benefited by the introduction of his streamlined control for the management of major schemes. Roger du Toit, an architect with a persuasion towards planning, joined in 1966, thus strengthening that aspect of the work. The reputation of being able to organize and complete extensive undertakings within time-limits brought further large-scale commissions to the office. The major development scheme for 1967–68 was Metro Centre, Toronto.

Weldon Library

This project involved the development of the run-down area over and around the train tracks of the Canadian Pacific Railway Company and the Canadian National Railway as a commercial, housing, and public zone, that blended the structures and open spaces with the transportation network. The passage of individuals and vehicles formed the basis of the planning. The established routes, connections, interchanges and links determined the placement, size, and nature of the proposed buildings. Unlike fanciful Utopias, Metro Centre was a hard-headed commercial venture. Its design followed a logical sequence of development: analysis of the problems, social requirements, economic and political realities, physical factors, and then formulating a solution. Far-sighted, radical, yet pragmatic, the Metro Centre proposal must be viewed as a major statement of Andrews' belief at that time in the future urban centre as a multi-level integrated complex.

The centre was to be efficient, with high utilization of land, and yet it had to accommodate a variety of activities and allow for individual choice of participation. The daunting scale of the proposal was too much for even the progressive Toronto citizens to accept. Interest-group protests, dissent between the major landholders, and ultimately the financial plunge, prevented the realization of the scheme. The Canadian National Tower stands as the single monument to the dream that was Metro Centre.

The CN Tower was designed not simply as a communications station, but as a focal point for Toronto, and specifically Metro Centre. While Metro Centre does not exist, for Toronto the tower is successful. Besides its monitoring function it provides local and visiting tourists with recreation, observation and dining areas at the various levels. The building is a progressive engineering design in pre-stressed concrete that impresses primarily because of its size. An earlier design in which the functional areas were elevated on fine triple supports was a more poetic and distinctive, though less practical, solution.

Metro Centre's place in history is akin to that of Scarborough. It came very close to realizing the shared vision of the sixties – the revitalized urban core arising from a new infrastructure that accepts what exists but adapts it to the demands of the present.

Main foyer

Concrete textures

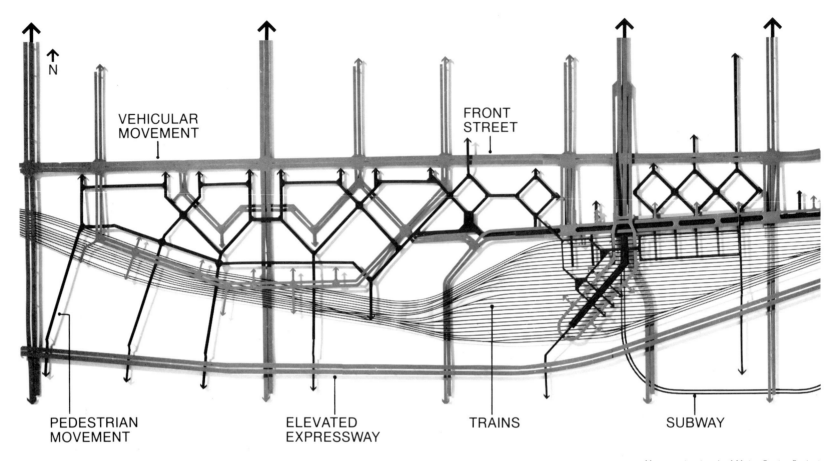

N

VEHICULAR
MOVEMENT

FRONT
STREET

PEDESTRIAN
MOVEMENT

ELEVATED
EXPRESSWAY

TRAINS

SUBWAY

Movement network of Metro Centre Project

Metro Centre

Metro Centre was a very obvious job. It was right under everybody's nose. The publicly-owned Canadian National Railway and the privately-owned Canadian Pacific Railway had pushed across Canada and had been given what land they needed, where they needed it, and obviously anywhere they made a stop a settlement of some description resulted. Towns developed around the railway tracks, particularly where the tracks ran together. (They divided on occasions, such as when they took different routes over the Rockies.) Banff is a Canadian-Pacific town and Jasper is a Canadian-National town but generally the tracks parallel each other, particularly around the lakes areas. The city of Toronto grew around the railroads and railroad holdings which, with all the marshalling yards, were substantial.

Eventually, it became impractical for the railroads to continue to use their yards, 200 acres in extent, in the middle of a city of two million people with its transportation problems and the blockage created by such a vast area of land. So the marshalling yards were moved north of Toronto, leaving only the passenger trains entering the downtown area. I guess real-estate pressures made the two railroads formerly mortal enemies, think it might be sensible to talk to each other and in so doing they decided to redevelop their now unused land.

Organization of the project

A joint venture company between the two railways was set up. This company was privately-owned, 50 per cent by Canadian National and 50 per cent by Canadian Pacific. The Board consisted of members of both railroads. To organize and manage the development, the company hired Community Development Consultants, headed by Stewart (Bud) Andrews. He eventually became the President of the joint venture company. Bud provided organizational know-how: how to find the right people to do a particular job; how to handle the political situations; and how to make the necessary moves in order to get the feasibility studies, program and design stick-handled through the four levels of government.

Bud Andrews had the responsibility of organizing the scheme, one of the largest urban redevelopments ever contemplated. He had to select the consultants. Every architect in Toronto was anxious, and not only those in Toronto. There was a hell of a lot of lobbying and the best lobbying we ever did was to stay out of it. We knew we had reputation enough to be approached by him if, as announced, he was thoroughly investigating all possibilities. The silliest thing we could do was to go hammering on doors so we just sat and waited and, sure enough, he turned up. We sat down in our little boardroom, just he and I and a couple of others from his outfit and from mine. His first words were, 'Why the hell should I hire you?' My immediate response was 'I'm not so bloody sure I want to work for you!' Bud Andrews later told me that in that minute he felt he had his man. It is just that sort of encounter, quick, and with a bit of fur flying that results in a high degree of mutual understanding when the air clears.

We were appointed as Architects and Urban Designers. Planning to me is that coloured pencil stuff. Now this was really three-dimensional – it had to be. It was not just making in this project areas for housing and arranging servicing zones for them; everything was on top of the other thing, so it was more or less architecture from the word go.

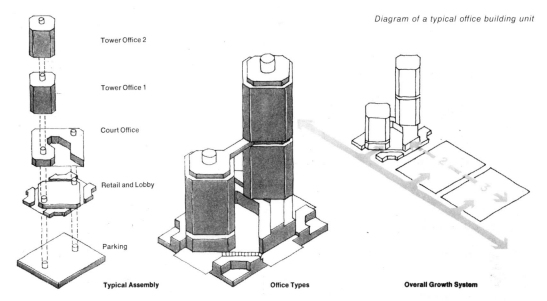

Diagram of a typical office building unit

Tower Office 2

Tower Office 1

Court Office

Retail and Lobby

Parking

Typical Assembly   **Office Types**   **Overall Growth System**

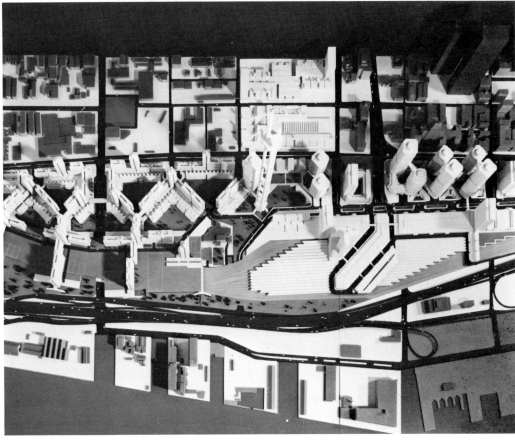

Model of original proposal

Community Development Consultants selected their own planning people but those planners were very much involved in the legal aspects and finding out where all the services were. The planners were where planners ought to be in my opinion – they were providing the information for the people who can work three-dimensionally. There were lawyers, there were surveyors, there were railroad men from both railroads, guys who knew about switches and knew about the problems of shunting trains and things of that nature, there were transportation consultants, there were structural engineers, mechanical engineers, electrical engineers – there was the biggest collection of consultants you have ever seen in your life. It was Bud Andrews' job to co-ordinate the project, but it was my job to co-ordinate the consultants, not make sure they did their work – he did that – but I had to co-ordinate and synthesize their input. It was the classic example of the architect's real role: the assimilation of the information provided by many and various experts, and the synthesis of that into a three-dimensional result.

Three or four people from our office were put on to the project. Roger du Toit, who had an architectural and urban design background was in charge when I was not there. We set up a little cell in Bud's office which was a mile or two from our own. It was a place where nothing happened but Metro Centre. I had three or four guys in there, others had a few guys in there, Bud had a couple of guys in there, the railroads had a guy or two in there, so there was a team of about 12 people. Roger du Toit was the co-ordinator of that group. The way it worked was that we had a formal meeting once a week where the previous week's work was presented, analysed, discussed and the next week's work was planned. Although I did not Chair the meeting, generally I presented the material. I went to that office at various times through the week, maybe every day, just for a part of the day, to see what was happening and to make sure they were doing what was supposed to be done. It was highly organized and worked very well. The end result of the nine-month study was the Metro Centre technical publication.

Andrews was the prime consultant and I think quite properly. We were a pretty good team. He would go and drink with the politicians and that sort of thing. He would have them into his office and he worked his way through the lot of them, week after week. I would come about 5 o'clock or maybe 5.30; they had been there since 4.30 or so, and usually had had three or four drinks. Coming in late I was three drinks behind, but clearer of mind. I would meet them all, and maybe we would just sell one little thing, like whether we would be able to extend the loop of the subway – it already had a loop but the sensible thing was to be able to take it a bit further. You really learned that in that sort of a situation it is a long job. You cannot just make drawings about it and do it. It is a whole process of getting together with people and letting them see what you want to do, and doing it gently. It took a long time but finally we got all the way, always with officials believing they had discovered the idea themselves – part of the performance.

The problem
The brief was straightforward – to prepare a master plan for the redevelopment of the railway yards. It was Andrews' job and ours to decide what it should contain, what was needed, what was marketable, what it would cost, in what order it should be built, and what the needs of the railroads were.

There were tremendously varying projections as to the future of rail transport. At that time they were frigging around with that turbo train from Toronto to Montreal and projecting a vast upsurge in inter-city train travel between Chicago, Detroit, Toronto, Montreal. At the same time they were introducing something called the Go-transit with surface trains to the surrounding metropolis.

It was an intensification of everything you can imagine. There were hundreds of trains of all types, long-distance, or suburban, or underground, and those trains disgorged thousands of people. In the future it could have reached pretty close to one million daily, and

there were probably the same number of cars. There were buses, again all types whether they be inter-city, inter-suburb or local. Island and lake boats connecting to the United States were also docking nearby.

Nobody said how each part would relate to the others – that was for us to figure out. They do have distinct relationships. Distance trains are very long and have carriages with lots of people in them and you have to get the people off the train as comfortably as possible, but it becomes centralized because tickets have to be sold somewhere.

There was also the Go-transit train, on which people commute to work every day. For this tickets can be bought monthly or yearly, so sales from them need not be in a central place. You can get off that train and disappear down a hundred holes. Then there was the underground which is more like the long-distance train because movement is not predictable. Some people catch it to and from work every day, other people use it irregularly. That also requires a place to collect tickets.

Then, where do you go from a train? To a taxi, or to another train. Then there were the long-distance buses. They had to be handled in a somewhat similar way. Where do you go from the buses? From a bus to a train, to the underground. Or by bus to the airport.

And then there were people. A lot of them who, when they come out of any one of those things, are going into the city on foot. It is a very complex business when all those modes of movement come together at the one point. They were already there but incredibly confused. Our job was to bring them all together, refine the system and try to make it work. Nobody was able to tell us what to do. We had to find out.

I do not know that it was all that different from any architectural problem, only the scale was enormous, it was a super-movement system. Later it did become eight million square feet of office space and nearly 10 000 living units, a convention centre, two or three hotels, staff facilities for both railroads and their own office space. It was an enormous development, including of course a complete transportation centre. This was making a substantial city related to all forms of transport. Really what we were designing was a master plan for Toronto and that is where it came unstuck. Once the powers that be were aware of the potential influence of the Metro Centre plan they got cold feet.

The solution
The things that are predictable are the things that you plan to end with. What we came up with was a three-dimensional urban movement system which was valid for as long as vehicles have wheels and people have feet. It was a reasonable assumption to think that things will have wheels for a while. We could imagine that the form of motive power might change, but probably the wheel business would not. It does not matter whether it will be a train as we know it or not. Or a car as we know it. But it will be a personalized capsule that holds one or more people. Also people will walk. They have walked since evolution and, although things move faster now, people will probably always walk. Now those things are predictable; you know about them.

The things that are unknown are the requirements for office space when it is conceivable that people may work at home in the electronic age. In most instances it may only be their need to get together, a social need, that will continue to motivate them to travel to work. This is unpredictable. The type of living accommodation – that also is unpredictable. One year you read that hotels are a wonderful business and the next year all the hotels are empty. Maybe we will not have hotels in the future.

There is no existing street system in a set of marshalling yards. Any roads in the vicinity of this one were not at the same level as the railway yards; in some instances they went over and in some instances they went under and by and large they were retained and reinforced. Our plan did not change the

existing motor car system of Toronto other than to allow the motor car to become involved in the other modes of transport. We had to provide the opportunity for the motor car to make its connections to the public transport.

I saw the movement system as being the basic structure. I could not have cared less where most of the things went within it. I did not have to self-consciously plan or design the system, but certain things happen when two systems cross. For example, where the underground went underneath the Go-transit and there was a need for people to go from the Go-transit to the underground, there would have to be a station. And when there was a need for people to go from the Go-transit to the long distance trains, or to the Greyhound buses, there would have to be more than a station. All we did was relate the needs of the various transportation or movement connections.

Toronto had any amount of open space. Its major visual open space was the lake and its major recreational open spaces were the Toronto Islands. Although the lake was there, it was inaccessible and could not be used by people who lived in urban Toronto. This problem could be solved by making Metro Centre serve as a connection to the lake shore. Toronto, because of its climate is a troglodyte town and there already existed a number of underground pedestrian links that came to a stop at the railroad track. The threads just had to be picked up and woven into an extended network. The lake shore was not originally part of this project but making a connection to the shore of the Metro Centre could influence later shore developments.

I did not see the problem in any predetermined way like Corbusier's Paris plan, or everything going up in the air by elevating roads and elevating buildings to obtain maximum green space. I saw it as solving the problem for Toronto and making a major contribution to the enjoyment of its inhabitants. Another pressing need in downtown Toronto was for intimate urban spaces; the little spaces where people could go and sit in the sun and

eat their lunch. They were not too worried about chucking footballs around or riding horses. Consequently Metro Centre itself contained many small and pleasant outdoor spaces suitable for small group activities and passive recreation.

The scheme was people oriented, as it is people who do the moving whether in cars, trains, buses, boats or on foot. Every time they move convenience is the thing they are after. That is what we came up with and that, as far as I am concerned, is the master plan.

Hassles
The trouble comes when you have to deal with presidents of railroads and board members of railroads and bloody councils, and parliamentarians who have not been educated beyond the fact that a plan is a model, is a picture, is an image, is a vision of what is going to be. There is no real point in talking about open-ended planning and things like that. You have got to show them something so they can say, 'Oh! Gee, that's ours' – something that looks real even though you are really trying to sell them an organization framework capable of many physical interpretations. It is unfortunate. You know it is wrong but it is the only way to get the plan approved. And I suppose, in one sense, that is also where we came unstuck, because as soon as that three-dimensional deal is made (and it *was* made, there was a model representing the transportation terminal) as soon as that was made the critics could come and say it was too strong, or it was too overpowering, or a piece of tenuous history was threatened.

The model did not show the retention of the great hall of Toronto railroad station so there were 12 months of incredible furore. People took sides, for some thought Metro Centre was going to destroy the railroad station. Maybe it was, maybe it was not. It was not saved in that three-dimensional plan, but the movement system would have allowed it to stay or go. I knew the model was the problem but I could not convince the next level, the prime consultant, that we should leave our options open.

Comment

In retrospect I think it was handled the wrong way in that all the guns were fired at once. We would have been able to get people to understand the reorganization of the railroad, and of the departure points from the Gardiner Expressway, and feeder buses – just bits and pieces. It was this big super bang of the presentation model that they reacted to. I got lost at that time. I was absolutely not supposed to go to Australia in September 1968 for the Belconnen job. The bang had gone off and anytime we were going to be into design on Metro. I said, 'Look, I'm only going to be in Australia about a month'. They said, 'Hell, what are we going to do?' I said, 'Give me a call and I'll come back early'. That was eight years ago and still no call. I am disappointed for the sake of Toronto.

There is no possible way we, as an architectural firm, could have built the complete project. I would like to have done the transportation terminal. Others could have built the bits and pieces but we could have maintained planning control and generally made sure that our plans worked.

The Metro Centre plan was no different from Scarborough in terms of attitude, but in terms of scale it was just *so* monumental. The office building system of Scarborough accommodated growth. It tried to look at and handle aerial subdivision, allowing pieces of buildings to be owned by different corporations and made provisions for aerial connections between adjoining buildings. The projected office densities were such that movement 20 storeys in the air was reasonably logical. Similarly, the office building component of Metro Centre that we looked at and figured out, was reaching forward in terms of putting buildings in cities.

I have always valued common sense. The Metro Centre project could not have been handled by anybody who did not have this because there are some absolutes that are unarguable. For instance if you do not put the bloody underground underneath the rapid transit and have a connection between the two, it will not work. A station down there,

one up there, and one over there, will not work. Nobody can argue about that. But the eight million square feet of office space, the 10 000 living units are completely incidental to the organization of the prime movement systems for Toronto. I think I have demonstrated through damn near everything I have done that I always approach a problem from the point of view of movement, be it only people on foot or any combination of people and vehicles. Movement is the determinant of any form of organization.

The Tower

Maybe, in a way, it is a good thing that Metro Centre never got built. I do not know. They will argue and fight and have committees and screw around for another 20 years now. Probably, nothing will ever happen.

The only physical manifestation of what amounted to five years' work and a hell of a lot of thought and energy is Canadian National Tower, a communication tower – the tallest free-standing man-made structure in the world. Its major purpose was to handle, in one location, all the communications in southern Ontario. Quite a sensible idea really, instead of having towers stuck up all over the place like pins in a cushion. Admittedly it does have a few bars and a revolving restaurant and a viewing platform and things like that and it will function as a communication distribution centre. This tower is the only built structure I have discussed in this book with which I have not been personally involved throughout. I have mixed feelings about it. It was an early study that was later reworked. It is not the tower I wanted to see there, it is not the tower that was supposed to go there, it is the tower that came after I had left Toronto, and although I was responsible for the concept, the detail design was done by others.

In the designing and building of the Canadian National Tower the relationship between the architect and engineer was very close. The architect created a form that would work for the engineer. Its design was a unique sort of a problem, because in order to function properly and be able to use the surface of Lake Ontario

The Canadian National Tower under construction

Model of the early scheme showing the three legged tower

View from the lake

for ground signals, it could have no greater movement than six feet. Being 1800 feet off the ground, that in itself was a monumental engineering problem, for which there were no precedents. The other very significant problem was the control of ice formation. It is alright for the Russians to build a tower out in the boondocks where bits of ice can fall off without anybody getting hurt, but we were building, right in the middle of the downtown metropolis, a thing that because of its height could collect ice for most of the year. Falling pieces of ice have a habit of damaging people's heads, particularly if they fall from about 1800 feet. That was one of the most telling design determinants. We therefore had to have completely smooth surfaces which would not collect ice. To further ensure that ice formation was impossible we used the heat generated by the transmission equipment which was working all the time and generating an enormous amount of heat. Instead of extracting the air and cooling it for re-use as in a normal air-conditioning system we used its heat to clear the upper section of ice.

The original design of the tower was a three-legged thing; the legs were connected at various stages, at the base they were spread apart. One leg carried elevators, another stairs, and the third services. The tower that was built has one leg with a tapered form. It was built as a continuous slipform. The concept was that once the slipform started it did not stop and the tapered form could be achieved by just moving in the ends of the formwork. However construction was stopped at weekends because of the unions. The tower has all sorts of exciting aspects like glass elevators going up the outside. I am not sure of the value of that but it certainly is quite an experience.

The city refused to give us a building permit so we just started to build it and nobody said 'Stop'! I have often thought it would be an interesting building to demolish.

Building a belief

Towards the end of 1968 Andrews was invited by the Australian National Capital Development Commission to undertake a large office complex outside the capital, Canberra. His practice was heavily engaged and the turmoil that was Gund Hall was at its peak. Gund Hall, the Harvard Graduate School of Design, has been a controversial issue since its conception. Andrews' selection as architect from past graduates of the school was a compliment that was not always easy to live with. From the beginning the project was rocked with strife and dissent – a predictable circumstance for any building designed for present and future architects. Even under normal conditions this would have been a hazardous undertaking, but the situation was worse than usual in the case of Gund Hall as it was commissioned at the time of the height of student unrest in America. Grasping on to the generously endowed Graduate School as a scapegoat, the students attempted to stop the design and have the money directed into community oriented programs. This well-intentioned protest did not make the architect's already difficult job any easier. In view of the circumstances it is remarkable that Gund Hall emerged in its final form as such a single-minded solution.

Gund Hall, detail of the studio

Gund Hall is Andrews most explicit building. It directly and simply insists 'there shall be no separation of disciplines'. In this belief, that is so eloquently and unmistakably stated in the building, Andrews was supported by the then Dean, Josep Lluis Sert. The building consists of three principal sections arranged around an internal street, originally intended to be open for general campus circulation, and to invite those from other disciplines to become, if not involved, at least aware, of the workings of the design school. Deprived of its intended use by the increased need for security, the through-route of Gund Hall remains as a misfit entrance hall. But with this building Andrews appears to have been primarily concerned with space rather than circulation. The three major components, the Loeb Library, the Piper Auditorium, and the studio, differ strongly in character. The *raison d'être* of the building is the great space of the studio with its stepped levels to rushing sloped tubular trussed roof overhead. Andrews has described the space as the 'last great railway shed' but it is not a railway shed. The enclosures of railway tracks and platforms provide an envelope for the large-scale activities taking place within – they are remote and neutral. The roof of Gund Hall is low, demanding and involving. It forces an awareness of itself and what it stands for. Principal debate has evolved over the central idea to which this building deliberately addresses itself, and its successes and failures towards the realization of that aim.

Here Andrews rejected the heavy walls of his previous works and replaced them with columns that clearly relate back to the early work of Corbusier. The offset section is built on a flat site and the triangulated studio section is sheathed in a brittle skin of blue glass. For Andrews this was a new sleek idiom, yet its refined external appearance belies a toughness that has adapted well to the stresses of occupation. Working shelters, chained bicycles, tents, plants, all join in the cacophony of use that the great shed was designed to accommodate.

With Gund Hall Andrews deliberately threw down the gauntlet, and even those most opposed to what this building represents, admire it as a brave statement from an architect with belief in his solution and the determination to bring it to realization.

The studio

Pedestrian approach

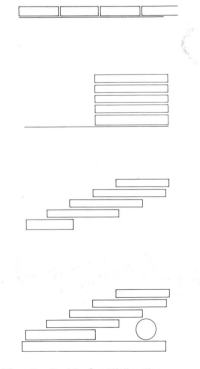

Diagram of the rationale of the Gund Hall section

Gund Hall, Harvard

Gund Hall

The Graduate School of Design at Harvard was housed in five buildings dispersed around Cambridge and included a factory and a basement. Our project was to design and construct 'George Gund Hall' the new home of the Graduate School of Design. The budget was $5.2 million; the building site was an area of land on the corner of Quincy and Cambridge Streets, just outside the Harvard Yard.

The Dean of the School, Lluis Sert, was potentially a strong client, but because of his forthcoming retirement he chose not to intervene in any consistent way in order that he might not impose his views on his successor. In that respect Sert acted properly. In a more pragmatic sense, his lack of intervention created a vacuum of authority which was never filled in an orderly manner, and this created a considerable number of difficulties for us. There were forty designers on the faculty, each of whom knew in his heart that he should have had the job, and what the solution should be. In addition, the Harvard Planning Office was filled with architects and engineers who were not bashful about insisting on their own pet ideas. Others concerned in the project were the administration, the donors whose consent was necessary to make the building possible and the students who knew exactly how things should be done. Each of these groups was 'the client'. There was no organizational structure to bring these diverse factions together. Working with each and trying to weld some minimal consensus amongst them became a wearying business.

In theory, the Building Committee was the logical agency for this, but it rapidly dissolved into outright obstruction in the face of student activism.

Originally, the faculty of the School had recommended to the Harvard Corporation that the architect be selected by competition. The Harvard Corporation decided, however, to select the architect itself, and did so without informing the faculty either that their recommendation had been squashed or that I had been retained. It was not the best of beginnings.

The problem

Ostensibly, the program prepared by the faculty was a highly developed, sophisticated planning instrument. What it lacked were meaningful statements about the philosophy behind the new School or the purpose of the building as the environment for a set of educational activities. If the zoning had allowed for it the requirements could have been fulfilled by a ten-storey building covered by ivy, with a bump in front for the library. The program contained all the necessary words, without substance. Under the heading 'Environmental Aspects of Studio Space' was the requirement that each studio contain a sink. Disregarding the academic jargon, it read like a catalogue of existing spaces. This transformation of the commonplace into meaningless expertise is symptomatic of the malaise of contemporary architecture; words and posturing in place of thought.

The finality with which the program was presented disguised a multitude of divisions amongst the faculty over what the School should be. There was no explicit consensus on what made the Graduate School of Design tick, no reconciliation of the powerful vested interests in the School.

With this lack of consensus amongst the faculty it became necessary for us to develop our own program for the building. Our basic goal was a building which reflected the integration of all aspects of environmental design studies. There is no way landscape architects, architects or anyone else can operate independently in designing an environment. Contact amongst the disciplines is essential. This directly contravened the territorial ambitions of individual departments.

For instance, the landscape architects would have been most satisfied with a building in which they had their own box with a sign on the door that said 'Landscape Architecture', a place where they could stay without having anything to do with anyone else. The irony is that twenty-five years ago, landscape architecture was scarcely known outside certain circles and urban design did not exist at all as a separate discipline.

No one can possibly foresee what disciplines will be important to environmental design twenty-five years from now, or even ten. It seemed foolish to design a building based on a specific academic program at a particular time, especially for courses such as these. The building had to accommodate the unknown. No faculty or administrator was prepared to dispute these criteria publicly. We won that critical battle.

The architect has the opportunity to hinder or enhance a learning situation. Following on the criteria of integration, the building had to facilitate contact by bringing students, faculty and administrators into a physical relationship with each other which provided opportunities for them to develop their own informal learning and social contact as they chose.

The users' program called for separate faculty and student lounges. Instead, a series of lounges were installed outside the toilets. There are no staff or student toilets; only toilets for men and for women, and always side by side. Also the lounge spaces on each floor sit between the studio spaces and the administration offices. Toilets are not the most sophisticated or subtle instruments for enhancing social cohesiveness. But they are like the sun, absolutely predictable in the basic services they perform and the demands users make upon them. Even deans go to the toilet. Everyone will have to pass the lounges, which are primarily open, comfortable spaces. The faculty member will see a colleague having coffee there and stop for a chat, a student will nail him about his last lecture, the dean will wander by with the registrar. A student will try to hustle a girl from the typing pool. These girls, in their own way and activities, are as important to the environment of the School as is the dean.

An environment cannot be created solely out of juxtaposition of lounges to toilets, or refusing to allocate lounges and toilets on the

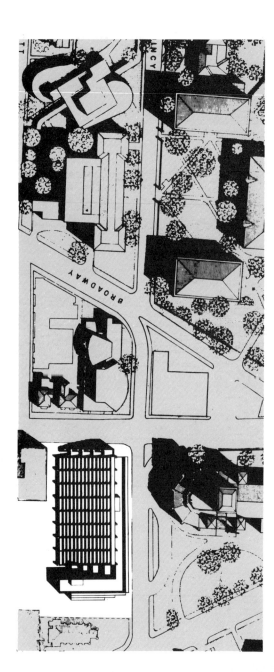

basis of rank. It is quite possible that subtle territorial distinctions will develop. The girls from the typing pool may tend to sit in one corner of a particular lounge space, the students in another, the faculty in another. That is the users' choice.

Of prime importance was the need for studio space on a small site. If all the studio spaces were on one level they would have more than covered the entire site. A multi-level building tends to separate people on different floors rather than bring them together. How could the activities of landscape architects be physically related to the work of the architects if the two groups were on different floors? How could the pressure of growth and change be accommodated within the rigid envelope of the conventional multi-storey building? There was no assurance that the space allocations decided upon one year would not be foolish two years later. It would have been senseless to have allowed ourselves to create future problems all because of a site limitation.

The solution
The solution lay in a design which avoided essentially irrelevant matters by the development of spaces in which everybody was, in spatial terms at least, equal.

It is a large factory-loft space with smaller spaces attached for specialized activities. To provide the amount of space necessary the studios are tiered like overlapping trays and covered by the single sloping plane of the roof. Part of each tray lay under the open roof, and part lies under the tray above. The rear part of each tray contained spaces for faculty offices, seminar rooms, lounges and the special activities which benefit from an immediate contact with the studios.

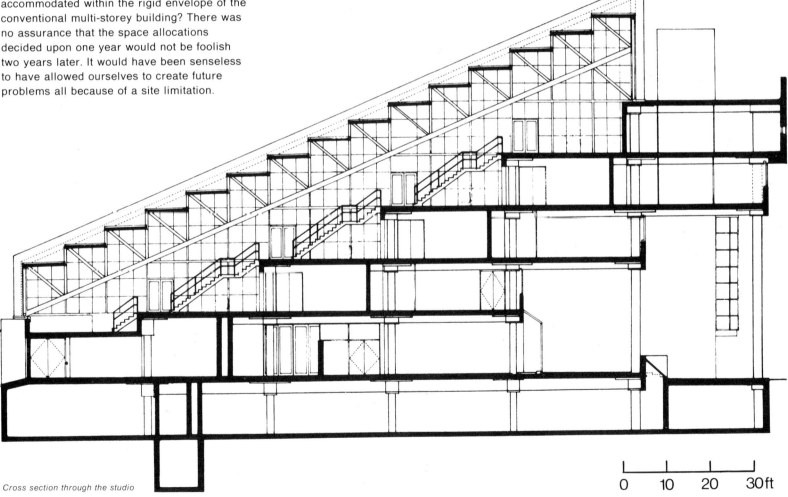

Cross section through the studio

0   10   20   30ft

The essence of the building – integration of disciplines, contact, equality, open-endedness, inquiry, flexibility – is represented by the arrangement of the studio space. A student standing on the top level can shoot a paper airplane to ground level and in the course of retrieving it discover all that is happening in urban design. It is that openness to simple curiosity, to inquiry, to cross-fertilization that the building represents. The open spaces are simple and undifferentiated and allow activities to be clustered in any manner found most suitable at the time.

The uncovered part of each tray is open studio space, visually and functionally connected to the other trays thus permitting students to have a choice. They can start at either end of the tray – extreme privacy or openness – and work towards a comfortable median; the choice is there. In that part of a studio tray covered by the tray above students and faculty who like to work in private can build their nooks and crannies. Architecture students have a predilection for self-created spaces and the schools at Harvard, MIT and Yale are riddled with them.

Throughout the design development the question of sound level was a major bone of contention. As soon as people saw the open space in plan they immediately assumed the sound level would be terrible. We carried out extensive acoustic tests to disprove this. Harvard hired its own consultants and their conclusion was the sound level would be quite comfortable, no more than in a quiet restaurant. This background of noise is itself part of what the building is about; it is the sound of activity of work and discussion.

No effort was made in the building design to separate academic from administration activities as these are often carried out by the same person. The distinction between the two kinds of activities is sometimes hard to draw. The conventional separation of administration from faculty and students lies at the heart of much that is wrong in universities today, and specifically at Harvard, as we later discovered. The office and meeting-spaces are set along the

western edge of the building and wrap around the corner to the northern edge, creating a strong connection with the lounges and studio spaces; this arrangement can be extended to the eastern edge if necessary in the future.

On the ground floor are the activities which belong there; the heavy work spaces for direct access at grade, the lecture theatre serving both Gund Hall and the University, and the main entrance to the library. Noisy activities such as power sawing are also located on the ground floor, but these spaces are sound insulated.

The rest of the ground floor consists of a generous amount of circulation space offering any student the opportunity to shortcut through the building and to become involved, at least visually, with what is happening there.

The idea of using circulation areas for exhibition space was derived directly from the experience of Scarborough College. The use of the ground floor, except for the library and lecture theatre, as one articulated circulation-cum exhibition area ensures the area will be continuously alive, even when no exhibition is hanging. It is also one marvellous place for a party.

The structure is column and grid constructed of poured concrete with an exposed finish. Cambridge sandstock brick is used on ground level and all the floors were to be endgrain timber. This wood was intended to contrast with the concrete and give it warmth, but this became a casualty of cost restraint.

At the heart of our difficulties with the faculty and administration lay, or rather sloped, the roof. It consists of spans of 145 feet with tubular steel trusses joined by secondary trusses glazed with flat roofs between. The roof covers the studios and creates the factory or arena form of space. Essentially it is a barebones roof structure.

Mechanical services ordinarily consume 30 per cent of a building's capital cost and, for that reason if no other, the services deserved

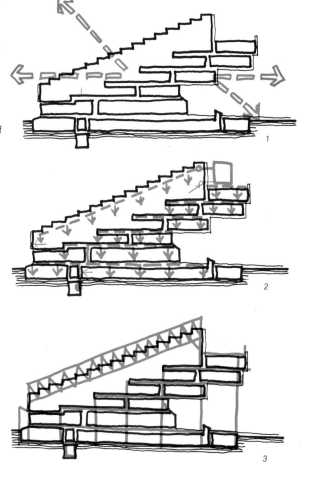

1 View and light
2 Mechanical distribution
3 Structural section

architectural expression in the School. Lying exposed, the mechanical services are easy for students to examine, easy to get at and easy to change, as almost certainly they will in the future, with no difficulty or effect on the structure. The roof and services provide useful object lessons about structure and services.

The building reaches to the extremity of the site. Given the original standard setback conditions and building height limitation, the potential volume of the building was reduced by almost 50 per cent. The solution was to tier the building so that it reached to the outer limits of the site at the upper levels but was set back at ground level.

The effect of this was to devote 20 protected feet of sidewalk width, the full length of the building, to the City of Cambridge and to the University. The overhang is sufficiently high not to be oppressive or to cut off sunlight.

North of the site is a small church which our large building had to treat gently. Because of this church there was a provision under a bylaw for a progressive setback at the north edge. Hence, the stepping-back profile of that edge which eases the building down to ground level. Under the terms of the gift from the Gund Foundation, the courtyard was to remain an open space. The studios face the courtyard and look out on to it through glass walls.

1 Library
2 Exhibition
3 Storage
4 Bar
5 Circulation
6 Lecture hall
7 Studio
8 Technology workshop
9 Janitor

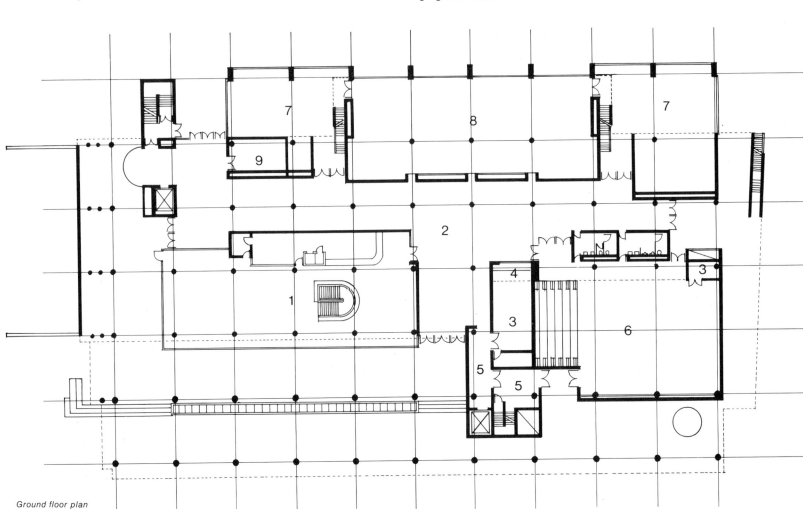

Hassles

Student disturbances were rocking campuses across the United States. At Harvard the administration had been doing a poor job for years. My sympathies were entirely with the students. When the activists assumed temporary leadership of the student body and struck out at the administration they chose the building as an obvious target; an alleged example of administration indifference to student needs.

A student manifesto was issued calling for changes in the building to meet contemporary requirements on campus. I had a great deal of trouble wrestling with the manifesto to achieve my own level of understanding of its meaning. In it the students listed a series of demands which, I had thought, were obviously our own design determinants. The manifesto set out the need to respond to the inevitability of change; to the social interaction amongst students, faculty and staff; the need to avoid designing a rigid facility which cannot be altered to accommodate changes in curriculum and course content; the provision of areas for the full spectrum of informal interactions; a major meeting-space astride the daily path of all members of the School; an 'interface' between faculty and staff offices and student spaces. It also insisted that the Harvard community and general public be brought into closer relationship with the School and that their interests be stimulated by making visible what is inside. These were precisely the objectives we had attempted to meet.

Ironically, the manifesto is the best description available of what the building is about. It was difficult to understand, in the light of what was obvious from the design drawings, why the manifesto was issued. Finally, I realized that it had been written in the context of student activism without reference to the actual proposed design or the objectives of the design. The manifesto included demands calling for an immediate halt to the production of working drawings, the possible dismissal of the architect and a fresh start. The manifesto was signed not only by students, but also by members of the Building Committee, including the Chairman, who had already approved the design. How the Chairman of the Building Committee and members of the Committee could, in the first instance, approve the design, and then turn around and sign a manifesto condemning it and suggesting we be fired is beyond my understanding.

The students and faculty called a mass meeting to discuss the building and John Simpson, Ned Baldwin and myself were commanded to attend. We were to respond to the manifesto and defend the concept. The meeting started at 4 p.m. I knew that sooner or later everyone would get hungry and their bellies would be more important to them than their principles. I stayed there for four and a half hours talking and answering questions until everyone had left. I was determined to leave last. It would be very difficult for the activists to organize students behind our backs if I saw this one through to the bitter end. That was a long day.

Even after that meeting had ended in a modicum of harmony and agreement, it was difficult to extract decisions from the necessary committees. The Building Committee in particular was so reluctant to commit itself in any way that the building was tendered and construction started without its written permission for us to go to tender.

Members of the committees appeared to be blind to problems with which, as professionals themselves, they must have been familiar. The original schedule called for the building to go to tender in February 1969. Faculty committees became involved in the small details of materials, types of lighting, whether tinted glass should be used – that argument went on for months. February came and went. New faculty came and presented new requirements which we felt obliged to incorporate, even though we had already fulfilled our contractual obligations for the design phase. Construction costs in the Boston area kept increasing, trade contracts ran out and new ones were negotiated. The client knew all this but was not prepared to compromise one modicum in order to keep within budget.

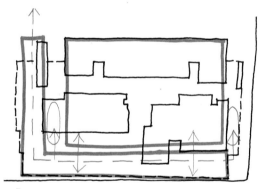

Adjacency diagram

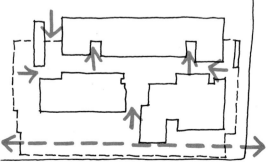

Ground floor access

Making a building is such a bloody intense thing in design time. It is all the way through you. It completely saturates everything you think about and everything you do. It was so hard – it meant dealing with so many different people and watching so many reactions of personalities and telling bloody lies, and manoeuvring so many situations. I suppose better educated or more refined people than us would maybe react in a different way, but I got drunk with joy so many times over Harvard. I will do anything to get what I believe in, built. Anything at all. We pulled all sorts of acts. We constantly needed to be intangible and in a position where they were not able to predict what we might do next.

On one particular occasion we rented a Cadillac (with a chauffeur) in Toronto and drove down just to give them the horrors and for no other reason. We had some sort of a meeting that went reasonably well and then we had a presentation that night at Hunt Hall. It was snowing like hell outside and we all got tight in Cronin's pub and decided to drive across Harvard yard in this bloody Cadillac. We got everybody upset and it ended up with a big snowball fight.

We just kept grinding away, and the pressure was incredible, so the release once we had achieved a little bit of a plateau was unbelievable. It was just a time to go out and have a really good meal. One particular time they were really giving us the jim-jams so three of us went and had dinner at Locke Ober's. They had signed a contract to pay our expenses. The dinner cost 103 bucks in 1968, which was a fair piece of change, and they really screamed when they got that bill. They then decided that was a bit rich so they adopted a new policy of travelling expenses plus $10 a head for dinner.

When the building finally went out to tender in July, the results were, as we had forecast, about $1.6 million over the budget. There were only two bidders, an indication of how bad the situation was. Because of the deductible options in the bids there was no legal way of determining the lower of the two bids.

Column details

Street colonnade and entry forecourt

At first the Harvard Corporation was determined not to have one of the bidders and favoured the other. It then decided to back down and call for rebids. It had recognized its responsibility in not heeding our warning forecasts of price increases, and admitted that the budget had been inadequate to begin with. It was agreed that the Corporation would provide an additional $750 000 to the budgeted cost and that we would knock $750 000 off the building costs. In effect, the capital cost was increased from $5.25 million to $6 million. In addition, the Corporation reimbursed us for our costs incurred in making changes after the design was approved and in politicking on the University's behalf. We then entered into separate negotiations with each of the two bidding contractors regarding possible reductions in costs.

The controversy over the roof continued. There is no doubt the roof constituted a significant proportion of the capital cost. The design was unusual and it had to be well built. The roof was also what the building and education was about.

There was paranoia and conspiracy in the air. At one stage Simpson was told not to bring me to the meeting the next week because there were a lot of people who did not want to see me. Apparently there were a couple of people who were really out to get me. It was as stupid as that. It was right in the middle of the time of the Harvard revolution. The roof became the symbol of frustration, anger and hostility. It is probably fair to say that ultimately the issue boiled down, not to the merits of the roof itself, but to who would give in – the architect or the opponents to the roof. We absolutely refused to back down, having been given no reasonable reason why the concept of the roof and open space under it should be abandoned. But I must confess that when pictures of snow in Boston appear on my television screen, I turn it off, just in case they pan across that roof and it is not there anymore.

Negotiations with the two contractors continued independently of each other. Assuming they kept to their word, it was likely on the rebid that the tenders would show a saving of $500 000 and would be only $250 000 above budget. On the day of bid opening, the first bid was approximately $25 000 over budget. The second bid was $25 000 under. The low bidder was the contractor the Harvard Corporation had refused to have previously. (Obviously, he was determined to build something for the University even if he had to risk his profit to do so.) Such are the factors which go into the design and construction of a building.

Comment

I think that Scarborough, Miami and Harvard, in North America anyway, are my best buildings and they were also the buildings that were the most fun to do. Intellectually and every other way Gund Hall had a much more significant effect on all of our lives than any of the other buildings – real total involvement with the pressure and the fun mixed together.

I went back once when it was about half-completed. We decided to have a cocktail party in the Parker House in Boston. We had a few people along, such as the contractor for the building, and Graham Gund, the donor. Gund and a fellow from the office decided they should make a presentation so they climbed up the flagpole on the hotel, took the American flag, and gave it to me. I had to walk around with a flag wrapped around me underneath my coat. But I still have the flag and I treasure that memento. For the opening ceremony we managed to find an equally large Australian flag, and made a presentation of it to Graham Gund. We even found one with a few holes in it and told him that they were part of the wear and tear of getting the bloody building built for him.

At the opening there was a party in the building. Both John Simpson and I were back in Australia by then but we returned for the party. I took my wife, four kids and my mother. To me it was a pretty important occasion – it had to finish with more than a fanfare and a couple of speeches. We had the biggest, loudest band in one corner and Harvard had one in another. We put on a sort of a Greek

The entry between the offices and the studio

Structure and services in the studio

meal and had a belly-dancer. We wanted to bring together again all those who had been involved in making the thing happen – even the people who had been a pain in the arse. The thing was there now in spite of them, and it was time to make amends.

Looking critically at Gund Hall I find I have more regrets than actual criticisms. Regrets that at times I was literally beaten into submission psychologically and was, with all the odds against me, unable to hang on to ideas which, in retrospect, were quite correct. There are two prime examples. One is the ground floor area where the original intention was that it would be an open circulation area which not only students, but the populace at large, would be able to walk through via the building, the theatre, the studio spaces, administration and library. Each were to have separate entrances thus introducing Gund Hall in a shopfront way to the City of Cambridge. This was not to be in the minds of the janitocracy, and closures were introduced providing security control at ground floor level. In retrospect there is no doubt the first idea would have added much to the design.

The second classic was that the original design called for adjustable louvres at the bottom and top of the big space giving opportunity for natural ventilation when desirable. Again the janitocracy held sway in insisting that students would open these windows at random and unbalance the air-conditioning system. In the aftermath of the Arab oil crisis with consequent substantial increases in running costs, the air-conditioning system is now not operated on weekends and never to the limit for which the system was designed. The opportunity for natural adjustment has been eliminated. The building is now too hot in the summer, a condition that would have been substantially relieved by the opportunity to introduce cross-ventilation through the studio spaces.

These decisions, of course, are never recorded and finally the architect must accept the responsibility for what is built. Therein lie my regrets.

And so to . . .

Before the construction of Gund Hall was completed, work had commenced on the preliminary design phase for the Cameron Offices in Australia. The Toronto weather, the signs of decline in the Canadian economy, the daily travel from Elora, the flights to Australia, influenced Andrews' decision to return to Sydney. The decision could not have been an easy one but he was prepared to take his chances for a better life for, and with, his family. In any case he had achieved his goal in America. The same challenges awaited in Australia.

Much of the success of the firm had come from Andrews' ability to attract creative and competent architects and to designate responsibility to them. When Andrews left Canada Ed Galanyk, who had worked with him on Scarborough, was holding the major responsibility for the Art Gallery and Studios for Smith College, Northampton, Massachusetts. John Simpson, who transferred from Page and Steele to the Andrews firm during the construction of Scarborough, was the designer for its second stage. Tony Parsons was engaged with Weldon Library and in designing the College of Art for Kent State University, and Ned Baldwin, Roger du Toit and Bob Anderson were involved with the Metro Centre and Tower program. A ten-man partnership was formed. With time Andrews' ties with the parent office lessened, and the partners in Toronto found it was not always easy to work under the Andrews name. Of the original partners only John Simpson, who now is a partner in Australia, and Galanyk and du Toit in Canada, remain connected with the firm.

College of Art, Kent State University

The Art Gallery and Studio, Smith College

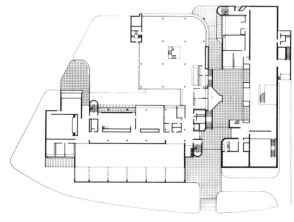

Plan, Art Gallery and Studio, Smith College

Australia:
King George Tower
ANU student residence
CCAE student residence
Cameron Offices
RMIT Library & Student Union

The new context

Perhaps the most significant aspect of the Cameron Offices commission is that it induced Andrews back to Australia, giving a fresh impetus to a sound but, for the most part, unadventurous local architectural profession. His Australian architecture reveals an uninterrupted development from the North American work. The economic, political and social context for architecture is similar in both countries. Geographic differences are considerable. These changes in climate and setting have modified the buildings' forms and led to a new relationship between closed and open spaces. Further, Andrews' increased experience and maturity are evident in his two major completed projects – the King George Tower, now American Express Tower, and the Cameron Offices.

Like Toronto, the profiles of Australia's major cities, particularly Sydney, were transformed during the building boom of the 1960s, but in Australia the financial crest occurred somewhat later, and was sustained somewhat longer than that in Canada. Consequently, when Andrews returned to Australia in 1969 both private and government funds were readily available for building projects.

First office at Palm Beach;
timber additions to the cottage

Against local advice the office was established not in the city, but 20 miles away from it, near his home at Palm Beach, a beautiful but distant seaside suburb of Sydney. Work on the Cameron drawings continued in the low-key unassuming office that was nothing more than a fibro-cement cottage on a hillside overlooking the Pittwater estuary. The informal, almost holiday atmosphere of the building, reinforced the intentionally relaxed mood of the organization.

During the initial years the Sydney branch remained small and there was much travel between Sydney and Toronto. Andrews often returned to North America and most of the Toronto partners visited Australia at some stage and contributed to projects in that country. The only permanently based Sydney partner was Peter Courtney who, as a resident Australian architect, initially collaborated with the Toronto firm for the preliminary work of Cameron. Courtney remained with the firm, and he and Andrews are highly complimentary partners. His sound legal approach made possible the development of the particular specification and contract documents that are major factors contributing to the innovative approach of the firm. While Andrews is the principal designer, it is Courtney who virtually takes over at construction stage and manages the operation on the site. Courtney's talent for architectural process and procedure relieves Andrews of major involvement in administration and supervision.

During the initial time in Australia the firm was committed to on-going North American work and the Cameron Offices and accepted no further commissions. But in the early 1970s they undertook two projects for L. J. Hooker, a large-scale private developer. One ultimately became the King George Tower, Sydney; the other the central city four-acre Roma Street Development, Brisbane, remained on paper.

Building in context

The commission for the King George Tower, located on one of the busiest retail intersections of Sydney, that of King and George Streets, presented Andrews with his first challenge to erect a tall building on an urban site. The structure is the most fundamental of twentieth century technology – flat slab on point column supports. The truncated triangular plan office floors are serviced by three cores placed on the apexes to allow sun, light and views for all sides of the building. Floor-to-ceiling glass walls are protected by a three-dimensional screen of polycarbonate sunshields that explode in a vibrant pattern, visually held and restrained by the dominant forms of the building frame.

King George Tower—polycarbonate sunshields

King George Tower is provocative and visually rich in the analogies it suggests. A local journalist's reference to the tower as 'a knight wearing sunglasses' is most apt, as this is a powerful yet romantic building, combining an almost primitive strength in poured concrete, with a fantasy of glass and contemporary lightweight materials.

The major contribution of the building to the Sydney scene lies not in the presence of the tower, but in the donation of the forecourt to the street-level activities. By setting the triangular tower in the rear corner of the site, Andrews has integrated the open space of the site with the footpaths and streets of the intersection to create an active urban plaza. Pedestrian movement patterns cross the site diagonally, and the street character is retained by the introduction of shops, bars and restaurants on the lower levels. With its acceptance – more than that, its welcoming – of the bustle of the city, the forecourt is a restless space.

The vitality of King George Tower comes from the evident conflict between the given program for exclusive office space and the architect's strongly held beliefs as to the responsibilities of such a building to its urban context. It is an inclusive and contextual building which, though not large in size, has an heroic quality. Here Andrews demonstrates even celebrates, the sympathetic integration of a tall structure with the urban mesh – a tenet previously stated in the Metro Centre scheme.

King George Tower in the urban context

King George Tower

King George Tower is the only building that has not come to me by way of an architect or an architectural connection. It really came up about 1965 when Keith Campbell, the Managing Director of the Australian developers, L. J. Hooker, was in Canada. He came to the office on a social visit and left saying, 'Next time you are in Sydney look me up'. On one of my trips to Australia in 1968 we had lunch together. By that time we had set up the office at Palm Beach and I explained that because of the Cameron Offices we were moving to Sydney. I was actually on the plane back to Canada when Campbell called Peter Courtney and said, 'We have a job at Milson's Point, could you do it for us?' Peter rang me in Canada and I called Campbell back saying, 'I'd like to do it but can't. I'm too committed to the Cameron Offices. If you come up with something else in a year or so I'd be delighted to do it.' And that is exactly what happened. I understand he was so impressed that I had actually turned down a major job that he shortly afterwards proposed we do King George Tower, albeit after I returned to Australia. The Milson's Point offices went to another architect who did all the preparatory drawings. I understand it was never built.

I can recall the first meeting on King George Tower. I went to meet the Australian Manager and New South Wales Manager of Hooker Projects and they asked if I would be interested in doing this building. I said that of course I was. Their response was 'Now, what we would like you to do is go away for three weeks or so and do some sketches as to what you think should go on that site in order to solve this problem and then, if we like them, the job is yours'.

I got up out of the chair and set off out the door and said, 'There is no possible way I would do that. I just do not work that way. When I put pencil to paper I expect to get paid for it.' And I literally did get up out of the chair and start out the door in a completely calculated sort of an act. That is the most important act. It is that very first time that is crucial. If I had sat there and said, 'O.K. I'll do that' from then on they would have called the

shots. As it was we did King George Tower on a full fee contract, but it all happened in one instant. You can imagine what was churning over in my guts as I walked away from a potential 20 million dollar job. It is the principle. You have had an education and you have spent a hell of a lot of time and money and there is no reason on this earth why you should work for a client and not be paid for it.

1970 was a boom time. Hookers were not only involved on the King George site, they had other projects going. They had the one next door, which is now Hooker House, but they sold that project before they thought of the opportunities presented by putting both parcels together. As the other building had not yet been designed we tried to persuade them to think of both projects together but it was too late, for while they still maintained the head lease and the project management, the actual happenings on the site were out of their control.

The site has a great location on the corner of King and George Streets right in the centre of the city. Its purchase was hotly contested by the major developers. I understand that Hookers and Lend Lease were the last two bidding and they more or less got together and said, 'Listen, this is pretty silly running each other up'. So they made a deal. The land by then had become some of the most expensive real estate in Sydney! I think it stood at about $400 per square foot, which is incredible. Hookers said 'We'll buy it and we'll give you the right to build it'. Lend Lease said 'Well, that's good for us because we have the construction company, Civil and Civic'. Hookers were the owners and Lend Lease (with Civil and Civic) were the nominated builders, so we worked pretty well from the outset with a builder, a situation we absolutely believed in and wanted desperately to make work. The only trouble was that the builders pulled out. It happened just in one day. There was a call from Lend Lease. 'Terribly sorry, but we really feel that due to our other commitments with Civil and Civic they will be unable to continue on as building consultants and builders'. We had spent months and months of detailed work and designed a building related to how *they* were going to build it. We then had to turn around and go back to the beginning and develop a set of documents to put a building out to tender. We were determined to lose as little time as possible so we introduced Hookers to the co-operative form of contract we were using on the Cameron Offices.

The Cameron document was refined. At Cameron it was being used for the Government so we had to make certain that every aspect of it was fully competitive. You do not need to do that with private enterprise, as private developers are quite prepared to nominate contractors they believe are capable of doing the job and they are not concerned about giving every contractor an opportunity to tender.

Peter Courtney is the expert on the contractual aspect of building buildings. He worked with a lawyer, and wrote the final head contract between the builder and the owner. It was put out to tender on the basis of profit, overhead, preliminaries and a bulk bill on the concrete frame. The successful tenderer was Sabemo. We had a builder.

King George was unusual for us in that it had to be more than five storeys high. Also, before this commission we had only worked with institutional clients.

Unlike institutional clients, Hookers were educated in the ways of building contracts, but this was their first experience, and our first commercial experience, in working this way with the builder. I think it was very good. Many of the design decisions which are quite often made without the advice of a builder and which end up giving both builders and architects real problems can be delayed. For example, because we did not have to specify the concrete finish in the tender, we were able to build prototypes of various concrete finishes.

Clients like that are nice people, but they are pyramidal in their structure and it is difficult to

stay in contact with one person for very long. They are moving around, they are moved upwards. We started out with one young man from Hookers and we really had a good thing going. Then he was moved to Malaysia and we finished up with somebody who was not involved at the outset. So we started everything all over again.

For a while, King George Tower was a good experience. There were younger people involved, albeit they were well down the line but there was tremendous enthusiasm and it really rolled well. It only came unstuck when the economy started to go down and there was not the room to move. The Hooker Corporation was retrenching people, so their people were feeling threatened, and when people are under any sort of economic threat their sense of humour disappears as does their desire to be in any way innovative or to take risks.

The problem

It is a strange shaped site – a surveyor's nightmare. Most cities, the ones that have been around for a while anyway, came from cart tracks and house lots and that is very obvious in Sydney. The site forms one corner of the busiest pedestrian confluence in the whole of Australia. When you think of Australia being 84 per cent urban, it is quite something

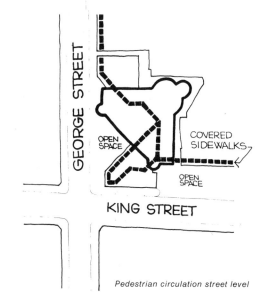

Pedestrian circulation street level

Below ground pedestrian system

to have the heaviest concentration of pedestrians in the whole continent at your front door. The site was originally occupied by a few rag-tag things but mainly by a department store that was an 'L' shape and went from one street to another but did not go around the corner. They had kept records that showed the number of people that cut across that corner via their department store. This had proved a very good merchandising device. We have tried to re-use that whole idea in the new development.

We ran into difficulties because King George Tower was designed at the time of the high mining boom and the tremendous desire of developers was to give their buildings a monumental image. The shops on the ground floor on that corner came after a long hard fight. The developers would have been happier with a great big marble plaza because, at that time, the wind-swept New York plazas trans-planted to Sydney carried prestige. But they were prepared to listen and go along with suggestions provided they made sense.

115

They were afraid of greengrocer's shops, with cabbages, outside the front entrance to a prestige office tower as they believed people would not rent space in a building like that. They were concerned that barrow men who sell cheap fruit and vegetables and who are on the run all day from the cops, might set up a stall there. I thought that sort of thing added life, and I really think that is tremendous. I would have them right outside my front door. But that is an anathema, or was at that time, to a developer trying to make a prestige building. The shops proved to be an economic proposition.

The site is half-way between the two major underground train stops in Sydney. It is half-way between Wynyard and Town Hall Stations and there is pedestrian movement between both of them. It is also on the way from Wynyard to the major departmental stores. Those that are left in Sydney now are lumped together in the one area, the so-called retail district. Once upon a time you could not have called Sydney a place that had retail 'districts'. But recent development has caused the financial district to develop because buildings have been built there that are the headquarters for banks and businesses and they have ignored what used to be Sydney's major characteristic – the whole ground level as one big shop.

The streets determine the structure of the City of Sydney. I think a lot of nonsense is talked about pedestrian separation. There are some nice things about slicing off parts of the city and making them wholly pedestrian and certain areas naturally lend themselves to this, but it can get carried too far. There is nothing wrong with the shot of adrenalin from dodging a motor car on a street, as long as you do not have to do it as a way of life. And there is not really all that much wrong with stopping the traffic and letting people cross with some lights and then starting the traffic again. It makes the city just that little less crazy. You get into a place like New York where the whole length of the Manhattan Island is timed on the lights and they can do 60 miles an hour up and down. There is a mad sort of pace to it, and Sydney is not like that.

The solution

The street links respond to convenient movement of people, not only between the railway stations, but on the way to most places in Sydney. There are some natural level separations resulting from the topography. The route of the old Tank Stream is to be used as a pedestrian passage according to the Sydney Strategic Plan. It happens to go right through this site but at a level below that of the streets. Because the stream exists, there was the opportunity to connect under the streets into one major department store and some other new developments. Those things all seemed to connect and their confluence happened to be the King George site so it was quite important to make a big hole, down from the ground level, to allow these lower pedestrian ways to connect into something – at the end of each one there had to be a spot of life and light.

The scheme tries to do a lot of things for the city. It is pedestrian-scaled around the bottom. There are one-storey places you can walk under and shop fronts and doors, not doors in glass walls 35 feet high, but doors in normal ceiling heights. The street levels are really about people walking around; across streets, along pavements, and around and through the building.

The main pedestrian direction is up George Street from Wynyard Station and turning left up King Street. If you can cut across that corner you can relieve the congestion at the intersection. That led to many things. It is also very difficult to build on the north-east corner in the Southern Hemisphere and make sure the sun reaches the southern face of the building. A lot of people looking at King George Tower would believe the pedestrian path across the corner determined the shape of a building 400 feet high! The tower facade and the concourse happen to be parallel but they have no relationship whatsoever. It is quite coincidental that the two problems are only capable of being solved in a similar manner. Striking at a 45 degree angle across the site allowed north-western sun to hit the south-western face and bring the afternoon sun to ground level in the open spaces. It is probable that future

Sunken forecourt

developments will build four-square to the street on the other corners; this has since happened on the diagonally opposite corner. But we have left one corner open to the sun and some penetration of light and sun can reach the streets.

The triangular form has another positive advantage; under the existing regulations, a setback had to be established from the major street when a building was built on a corner. The major street was the wider street; whether it be major in terms of traffic is of no consequence. King Street was the wider street therefore the height of the building and its setback would be measured from King Street. By having a 45 degree angle running back from King Street the height of the building was to the mid-point of the 45 degree angle and not to the edge.

You do not show a developer a triangular building when he has only ever been used to square buildings and expect his answer to be 'Terrific!' He is just not built that way. We had to do a study of every possible rectangular form on that site. It damned near needed a computer to put all the mathematical ingredients together, with the height setbacks, areas, nett to gross; but the end result is that King George Tower has, in its present form, maximized the area possibilities.

117

It has a building site ratio of 14:1. The allowable is 10:1 plus bonuses. But it took about a year to convince the developer. It is not really a triangular building, it is a rectangle with a side chopped off – square bays with columns at 25 feet centres and a 10 foot cantilever around the outside edge. The spaces are all big enough to be divided up in a normal rectangular way except that it became quite obvious that the major flexible component would have to be a partitioning system that was capable of running not only at right angles, but at 45 degrees to the facade so you could then get right angles, 45 degrees and 135 degrees. That enabled a much more flexible interior layout.

The building is structured only as columns and flat slab. It has an elevator core at the apex of the so-called triangle and two fire stairs at the other corners. The elevator core is a hollow circle enabling people to stand in the middle of it and see all of the elevators they may wish to catch.

Ground floor plan

←N   7.6 GRID

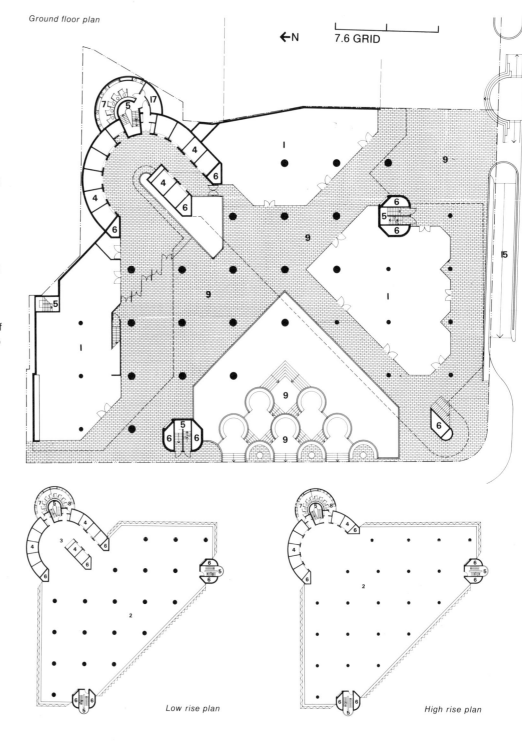

Low rise plan

High rise plan

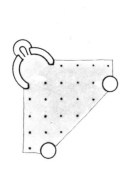

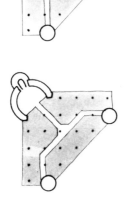

Subdivision possibilities

The building is 80 per cent efficient, that is nett to gross. In other words 80 per cent of what is built can be rented. That would be very close to the most efficient building in Sydney. Once you can get to that stage of the design then the developers will start to listen. They then begin to see the advantages, rather than only danger, problems and loss of profit, in an unconventional plan.

The decision to build in concrete was made when we were working with the first builder. It was the most logical material to use. We had off-street facilities so the trucks pulled off the street before the concrete was taken out. You could not have unloaded in George Street; it is the main street in Sydney. The use of cranes became a major design determinant. Only one crane should be used on a high-rise building. If two are used at $3500 a week, costs will escalate. Usually the crane is situated near to the centre so that it can reach in every direction. Therefore, it follows that the outside is normally as far away from the stem of the crane as possible. The great, heavy precast units that are commonly used in Sydney for sun protection are the heaviest load. It is illogical to put the heaviest load on the end of the boom of the crane. That is one of the reasons why we used very light stainless steel frames for sun-shading. It is one of the last things to go on and it goes on at the end of the crane. Therefore it needs to be light. That way we could get away with a much smaller crane; in other words, less money per week than if the heaviest load to be lifted was on the end of your boom.

The client was not familiar with board-marked concrete but was prepared to spend the money to build a three-storey prototype. The prototype served two functions. One was to display the type of finish and the other to explore how that type of finish could be achieved. We tried about 25 different types of boards or patterns as we went up. We found that obviously the quickest way was to slipform, but in slipform patterns cannot be made because the form is moving. We devised a method of slipforming with the outside form jumping a level at a time. It detached itself,

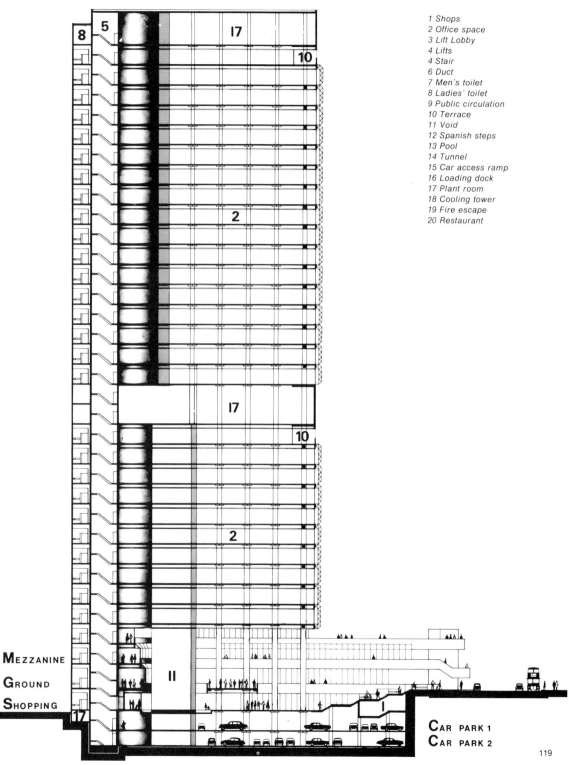

1 Shops
2 Office space
3 Lift Lobby
4 Lifts
4 Stair
6 Duct
7 Men's toilet
8 Ladies' toilet
9 Public circulation
10 Terrace
11 Void
12 Spanish steps
13 Pool
14 Tunnel
15 Car access ramp
16 Loading dock
17 Plant room
18 Cooling tower
19 Fire escape
20 Restaurant

Section

119

went up a level and came back again. That was a great system, but then the builder left and we had to go back to the start. The second builder proved that he could build more efficiently by the conventional gang-forming method, but with forms that could detach themselves and move up and come back again. So it was constructed by gang-forming, not slipforming. It is not a super-sophisticated structure. The elevator core, the two stair towers, and mechanical rooms at the mid-floor and at the top, form the basic frame and the rest of it is just floors held up on columns. It is not in the class of the Cameron Offices as a structure.

The columns were designed to be round throughout the building as this made structural sense and they could readily accept walls from various angles. An outside study convinced the people that make decisions that the columns in the office spaces should be square because of the tables and filing cabinets and things that would be put up against them. In making them square they appear much larger and the client spent more money than necessary, as all of the concrete outside the circle is superfluous. I take no responsibility at all for the square columns.

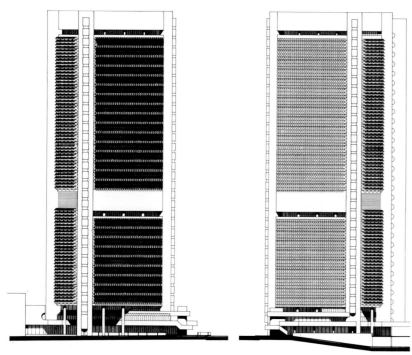

West elevation   *South elevation*

External frame supporting sun shields

The ceiling system comes from organizing the partitioning system to be both at right angles and 45 degrees. The ceiling is nine feet high, not eight feet, which is the minimum height, because of the vastness of the areas and the potential of the building to be used as open floors. It is of faceted metal pans with acoustic treatment behind. It is faceted just so that the ceiling itself is not simply a big flat plane but something that provides its own individual interest at close quarters. That is just part of being a little serious about the environment of the individual who will be in a place like that. It has a 'loo with a view'. We had to fight to get the toilets in a position where they could have windows with views of the outside. My feeling is that if you are in a vast building, would it not be nice if you could see the sun or the rain, or whatever, at least twice a day?

In a city building the size of King George Tower, someone is probably going to end up in an area where he cannot see the outside. One organization will put all the executives around the outside where they can get the view and the light, and the typist pool will be in the middle. Another organization will do exactly the opposite and put the working people where the light and the view is because their application is not as high as that of the executives. The usual solution is a building which has working areas where people cannot see the outside, and also places the services in the centre core.

The views are open from all the spaces apart from the rear of the third, fourth and fifth floors where the building backs up against the old Post Office. But they tell me that that part of the Post Office will be redeveloped.

A three foot space between floor level and ceiling is provided for structure and mechanical services. To make the building simple the walls are a full glass system with welded glass mullions floor-to-floor. All glass is beautiful detailing. We rejected the conventional solution of solid walls and then windows; that is house, not big building, technology. If you have two planes that are nine feet apart and a piece of glass will go between them, why not?

A lot of the problems in other buildings with sheer glass have been that people will not go near the glass because there is nothing outside. King George Tower has external lacework and the psychological problem of vertigo does not occur. Hooker's advertising man picked it up, 'If we can wear sunglasses, why not buildings?' He is quite right because we have moved away from concrete hoods that attempt to create some modelling of the surface and give some shade and shadow to all glass buildings. Technologically the heat that is allowed in by an all-glass building can readily be taken out by the air-conditioning system. The question that I put to myself was, 'Why do that sort of thing, it is unnecessary; you do not have to let heat and glare in in the first place?' There are such things as 'sunglasses' which prove quite adequately that protection does not have to be opaque.

King George Tower has a very light sunshade system. It was made in a factory and could be

lifted up on the end of a crane and put on the outside of the building. It is also fine enough in its complexity to form the ideal protection for window-cleaners. On every floor level there is a window-cleaning gallery as part of the sunshade screen so that the cleaner cannot fall off, nor is he hanging 400 feet up in the air on the end of a rope on a swaying platform trying to clean the outside.

It is more like a tree with leaves – it does not eliminate all of the sun. The corners of the polycarbonate and the stainless steel do not merge completely so you get little shafts of sunlight through. That gives a fantastic sort of pattern inside.

Australia has more sun than some places but I do not see this as a regional solution. The air-conditioning costs are less than half the normal amount because heat is not building up in the office spaces. Also the stair and elevator towers form part of the dimension of the exterior. With this layout the actual glass area is about 60 per cent of that on the usual square office building of the same floor area with the core in the middle and the glass all the way round.

From the interior the shades are transparent. They change colour slightly depending on the background. It is not a total screen. At least 50 per cent of it is open because the shades are angled. When you look out the view is patterned from clear to slightly grey or grey-green.

Comment
I am not fully happy with the final result. There are a number of things that could still be done. The finishes were cut back when the money became tight, things like the stainless steel ceilings that would have picked up the people moving through the concourse and reflected them. They should go back in. The ground level is still too formal for my liking. That is a hangover from the time of building the Taj Mahal for mining companies, or whoever were the people that everybody envisaged might pay $20 per square foot. A few cabbage leaves around the front door might not hurt.

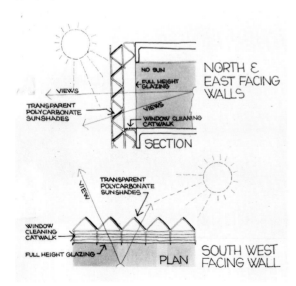

Conventional solutions

Campuses and colleges

The Roma Street Development, Brisbane necessitated the opening of an office in that city. John Simpson, who joined the Australian group in 1972, became the partner in Queensland. Although the project itself was never constructed, contacts made resulted in further work in that State.

The North American experience in university projects led to similar commissions in Australia. Master plans for future development were prepared for four tertiary education institutions in Queensland. Three of these were existing institutions whose status had been upgraded by government policy. The four plans emphasized the social needs of the students as well as their physical requirements. As with the plan for the University of Toronto, an attempt was made in all the master plans to unify disparate unrelated structures by sympathetic pedestrian routes and link spaces for informal gatherings.

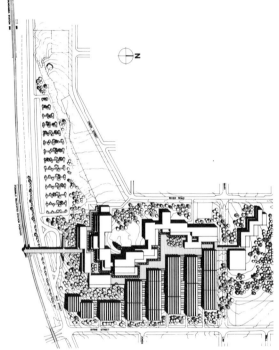

Master plan, Ipswich College of Technical and Further Education

Model, Roma Street Project

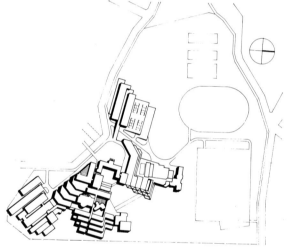

Master plan, Kelvin Grove College of Advanced Education

The organization of the work-load was typical of the firm, for while Simpson was the architect on the spot, planning was undertaken in the Sydney office with responsibility delegated to Doug McKay and Bruce James.

Smaller numbers of students and a more liberal attitude towards their freedom allowed for a more domestic format for the student residences of the Australian National University (ANU), Canberra, and the Canberra College of Advanced Education (CCAE). In these complexes the sexes are mixed and cooking and dining facilities are provided for each group.

123

The ANU residence is a low-cost structure intended to provide centrally located inexpensive accommodation for 250 students. The connected three-level building units are reached by individual vertical circulation – thus totally eliminating the institution corridor. The ten-person group's domain is fully protected from intrusion if desired, though connecting doors between sitting areas on each level do allow for horizontal circulation. Privacy increases with the distance from these doors – the sitting areas are adjacent to the entry, and the study-bedrooms are protected by the central position of the kitchen at one end and the stair tower at the other. The units are staggered on the periphery to allow for pleasant outlook and privacy. The ANU residences resemble the Canadian schemes in their small-group planning, and in the stark appearance of the exposed concrete and brickwork, but the type of accommodation offered is much more varied.

The CCAE residence is smaller, housing only 174 students. In its planning it went one step further by breaking the building-form into separately defined 'houses' for each group of six. The small concrete resident blocks with their curving corrugated asbestos roofs are stepped down the slope of a small hill to afford north oriented panoramas from each study-bedroom. The units are approached by uncovered paths up the slope which lead to direct access by individual porches and front doors.

The social organization breaks from that accommodated in the three prior residences. Each unit is independent and the public paths provide the spaces for further social contact. The scale and distribution of the units creates a level of intimacy more closely resembling that provided in general residential developments.

With all these schemes Andrews initiated fresh concepts for student housing, based on his North American experience. The domestic organization, and the freedom the design solutions afforded the occupants, provided a marked contrast to the institutional nature of earlier educational establishments built in Australia.

Student residence, Australian National University

Australian National University student residence

It started out as being a good idea. The Australian National University in Canberra wanted to combine a residence with a proposed centre for continuing education containing such things as seminar facilities. A suitable place for visitors to come to, and stay, and learn, particularly during the summer months and other off periods. That never happened. The residence was to be twice as big as it is today but it was chopped down to accommodate only 244; a frustrating evolution absorbing many months of planning and replanning.

ANU interviewed lots of people. We went along and did the old 'straw hat and cane' routine, and the University finally called up and said, 'Well, Mr Andrews, you will be very pleased to know the Board of Governors have agreed to hire you as the architect for the student housing' and away we went. It started out as a normal relationship. A very *avant-garde* committee, including students, was set up. It was quite traumatic to have a Users' Committee for a student residence that actually had a couple of students involved. It was the first time ANU had ever had students on a committee for a residence, let alone anything else. The students were fine but there were factions within the faculty. This was the first time anybody was actually *thinking* about residential accommodation. Previously they had just gone ahead and built residences, one for girls and one for boys. These all had bedrooms, bathrooms at the end of the corridor and a place for the high table and dining-room and kitchen – the world-wide traditional form of residence with no recognition of today's real social needs.

But this time several members of the Committee had been on overseas trips and had investigated many forms of university accommodation; all had different ideas about what should be done. We must have sat through two years of discussion. We had strong ideas ourselves and, after all, had been hired because we had previous experience in student residence building. It became a process of showing what university committees could look forward to in university residences in the future – residences that might be flexible enough to respond to changing social needs.

About this time large developers had begun to work their way into institutional situations with package deals wherein they would provide a complete price, a design, a completed building and everything else at a lump sum. They tried to take over. We managed to fend them off for a while and continued as the architects, but the seed was planted in the mind of the University that maybe they could get a cheaper job by the package deal method rather than the competitive tender. There were also other corners that could be cut. They realized that they could save 1.8 per cent of the cost of the building by not having the architect supervise it. After all, large institutions have three or four architects of their own on their staff. It was at this point that we, after having fully developed a set of working documents, lost control of what happened on site.

The problem

The site was a left-over space which was never intended to be used for any building; a long thin strip of land following the edge of a creek that has been running there since time began and had been filled and played around with. In fact, as we later learned, it was a bog in parts, requiring complicated foundation design. The best things about the site were the fine stand of weeping willows and poplars that followed the water, and its convenient location to the student union and other central facilities.

The traditional residences that existed at ANU were becoming increasingly unpopular having no opportunity for group living and being far too rigid and inflexible socially. A normal residence still treats students as children whereas society requires that they be adults. Apartment living was what students wanted, but on the open market, could not afford.

The brief did not go anywhere as far as our final design. It called for a central kitchen on the ground floor in which every student had a separate locker. The assumption was that

Axonometric

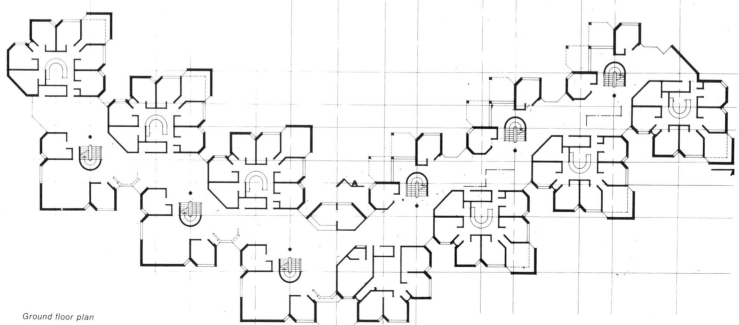

Ground floor plan

people cannot live together without somebody knocking off someone else's bread, or milk, or piece of steak. Late in the day this attitude was still evident – each refrigerator was supposed to have separate, padlocked compartments. We looked into trying to get them made, but we finally just put in standard refrigerators. Here there were groups of ten and that size presents few problems. Perhaps when you get into the larger groups the need may arise for the individual wire cages in the refrigerators.

The business of eating, or not eating, took months and months to resolve. The Committee was divided absolutely as to whether students should be able to cook in their rooms or whether there should be a kitchen and dining-room. Everybody wanted the smaller groups, but it took a long time for the non-student members of the Committee to accept that students could be allowed to cook for themselves and that they would not sit in a corner and starve to death. Above all they were concerned with the lack of surveillance. On the one hand you call people adults, send them off to fight in wars and let them have a vote and so on and then they are not even allowed to decide whether or not they want to eat. This concern goes even deeper. In the earlier colleges somebody makes the bed, and somebody sweeps out the room and tidies it up and cleans the bathroom. One reason we were really talking about this form of accommodation was because it had become too expensive to pay all those people on all those shifts to do all those things. And then you say, 'Well, couldn't they make their own bloody beds?' They say, 'Oh, but you know what students are like, they won't make the beds and will leave the same sheets on for weeks and weeks and then there will be vermin in the beds.' I replied, 'Well, so what! If they want to live like that, let them.' We really had to talk in this way for months and months and months to get the Committee to come to grips with the fact that they were dealing with adults and not 10-year-olds.

It really was not a case of being asked to design a low-cost building. It was a case of 'Students need more accommodation

desperately, but we cannot afford to build the type of accommodation we have had before, not so much in terms of its cost per square foot, but in terms of what we must charge the students to live there'.

This is when the whole business of maintenance and servicing comes under scrutiny. I think at Toad Hall they have a cleaning system where somebody goes through once a week. Maintenance is not totally left to the students but it is not like the old days. In order to continue the college system there needs to be more money devoted to building maintenance, provision of food and cooking operations than to amortizing the building.

The solution
It is a long building standing over an unenclosed street which can be entered anywhere along its length, depending on the way you are coming from the campus. You could not say there was a front door. The shape comes from the very long, thin site. Realizing it has to be long and thin you try to find a way to add some variation to its length so that you do not get the feeling of looking down a shooting-gallery – a bit of interest or variation.

It was originally designed to be built with terracotta block like Guelph but it was being priced when labour had gone crazy. You could not get bricklayers; you could not get carpenters; you could not get people to pour concrete, or anything. Material choice was a real toss-up for a while, not so much in terms of money, but in terms of available labour. The advent of a whole new team of bricklayers coming to Canberra swung the decision in favour of brick.

The foundations were difficult. They put down piers and built a raft that acted like a solid foundation to enable the brickwork to go ahead.

The outside form is crenellated – nothing to do with bows and arrows, but in order to get a minimum bedroom size with wall dimensions

Student accommodation

to take beds or things you may want to put against them; and putting them together in such a way that you got a window, sometimes vertical, sometimes horizontal, depending on the aspect and the sun. The methods of grouping needed to take into account the various needs of physical area requirements, social factors, functional operation, structural and building aspects, means of access and egress, fire requirements and cost limitations.

The study-bedroom houses a single bed, writing desk, wardrobe and easy chair. The splayed corners are dimensioned as the width of a bed and the long walls the length of a bed. There are several possible bed positions and, combined with four window types in the walls, the nett result is the possibility that each room can be different. In addition the rooms gain added individuality through their final position and orientation in the building plan. The room is seen as a private realm, unlike the one next to it or any other, where the student can retire to absolute privacy should he so desire.

In each unit one group of five bedrooms has a very close relationship to the kitchen. Another lot of five bedrooms has a very close relationship to the stair. Those two forms are rather similar. These ten share a lounge. A bathroom forms the connection between that group of 10 and the next group of 10, providing a sideways link. In cleaning your teeth you meet a different group of people from those that you might meet when frying your egg, or walking up your stairs.

The University wanted to mix the sexes but wondered how to do it and still not lose anything if it changed its mind while the building was under construction. If there had been a definite commitment to have mixed sexes we would have handled the problem in a different way, but the time of planning the Committee did not know whether mix of sexes would get past whoever had to pass it. The major concern was the possible sharing of a bathroom. It was as far as anybody had gone to have five girls over here and five boys over there. If the University wanted segregation the

girls' bedrooms could be round the stair and the boys' bedrooms round the kitchen. There are some double rooms but they are not really suitable for married couple accommodation. They are big enough to hold a double bed but I cannot see them being terribly successful as married accommodation.

Not wanting to dictate the absolute micro-environment we initially planned that rooms would be of a suitable finish to be painted each year by the incoming students. Thus they could decorate to their own choice; a lesson learned at Guelph, but eventually too radical for ANU. Of course, it is really up to the administration. You can strike some cranky supervisor who refuses to let the inhabitant do anything and then, too, you get the reverse – a student who will go and paint graffiti all over the inside and really make a rude mess out of it. You cannot be sure that people will be responsible with that sort of approach – and that is why administrators are not always prepared to gamble. Then you get inhabitants who just take it into their own hands and paint it anyway and suffer the consequences, if any.

Comment
The loss of control during building emanated from the ANU's decision to accept a builder's package, with no architectural supervision. The only common ideal in this sort of situation is the builder's desire to maximize profit with little or no understanding of the intent of detail, and the University's public service attitude of not causing trouble or work for themselves – 'get it done with the least amount of argument'.

I cannot pretend to be completely happy with the final result. Too many of the maybe small, but nevertheless important details were scrapped after Toad Hall ceased to be under our direct control. In our original plan each bedroom had a hatchway or peep through alongside the door to operate very much as the Oxbridge system of two doors, both closed means keep out, one open, one closed means knock and enter, I am home, without eliminating the essential privacy. The idea was not used.

I believe the lounges are probably too much of a thoroughfare with too much circulation. We had hoped they would be used as quiet backwaters.

All in all I think the social statement of Toad Hall is its success, being the first sizeable residence in Australia to change the student college concept – too bad it is not better built.

Ground floor street

Canberra College of Advanced Education student residence

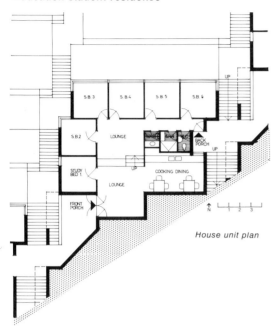

House unit plan

Pedestrian path between two groups of houses

Students' residence, Canberra College of Advanced Education, view from the north.

Canberra College of Advanced Education, a recent addition to the College of Advanced Education Program, had embarked on building student accommodation to keep pace with rapid student growth. Up until this time the residences had been built in the traditional architect/builder relationship.

For this residence the College called for what was known at that time as developer-proposal bids. They called not for a design – but for the submission of the names and testimonials of the builder and his team. He was the builder and we were the architects for the ANU residences which were under construction at the time. With the interest being taken in that project he could hardly lose, provided we went along in the team. Our relationship was with the builder and he paid us. This became a ridiculous way for an architect to practise. I know that now, and I will never work in that relationship with a builder again.

During the early phase of the job I went to various meetings with various people like the President, the College Architect, and a Committee for the residences, etcetera. We did the drawings; they approved them; and we went into documentation. At the end of our documentation period the builder was required to provide the College with a design and a price. Consequently, he was always there pricing what we did as we went along.

For instance the residence was designed as a poured concrete structure with an asbestos cement roof. This goes well enough together for a maintenance-free type of design. The builder absolutely insisted on changing it to brick. However, as he had given his price to the College on concrete the change would have caused all sorts of stirs so we managed to win that battle. But we could not make him do every little bit of the concrete the way it was drawn because we had no right of supervision, no right of control; the result is bad concrete and clumsy details.

The solution

The planning for the whole College had been done by the same people who did the architecture. This was the first building to be done by an outsider and this was the next piece of land that had been set aside for residences. I did not argue – I just put it there. The site was sloping, with a north face. There was not quite enough hill so we had to make a bit more. If you are building on a slope like that there are all sorts of advantages in terms of being able to see from one unit over the top of another and being able to tuck part of one unit underneath another unit and telescope the whole thing together.

This time we moved much further towards a group of 'homes' for students. They are really apartments with everyone having a single room. With this project there was no question about mixed sexes. 'It's a place for kids to live. If they want to sleep with each other we are not going to worry about it.' That was the first time I ever heard that said! Even so, the building was designed with an option for separating the sexes. If the College administration, in their wisdom now or at some later time, decides that this has been a disaster, the option is still there – it is a mistake to design a building that will work according to only one philosophy.

The site was relatively generous and we could get down to really making houses. Each one of those units actually has a ground level entrance, and it also has a back door and a front door, and just some of those little Hertzbergian businesses of stoops and places to stop and gather and meet. Your front door is quite close to another bloke's back door. Those things I think are very good – it really is nice to be able to do them. It was impossible to do that in the enormous scale of Guelph with the very, very tight conditions that pushed you away from ground level.

At CCAE we were able to use the ground all the time. The housing is accessible just like housing on a street but is much tighter. It has a hell of a density – about four or five hundred people to the acre. The stairs are outside so anybody can use them in a totally public way and visiting works very well. An extension of that is that it can start to make a college not

131

need a student union. The whole housing group becomes a student union. Not that it has billiard tables and ping-pong tables all through it as student unions do, but everybody is welcome there and that is all a student union is.

I have had student unions to design, but not build. They are only necessary as a more or less remedial thing in a badly planned campus where there is almost nowhere for people to go, or in a campus where some groups live on campus and other groups come to campus and you want to accommodate them in a situation where they can mix.

The bed-study rooms all overlook the view up the valley. They have been given priority in this respect over the sitting-rooms. I think this is logical as with the curricula today students probably spend as much time in their own place during the daylight hours as they do in the classroom. They come back there to do projects, study, and that sort of thing, but their use of the sitting-room and the kitchen is basically only at night – maybe the kitchen for a quick breakfast, but it is mainly at night that they are used. There is no real need for views from a living-room that you only use at night. Still, you do get a little bit of view from those rooms. I tried to get a fireplace for them. It

would have been fantastic if each one of those sitting rooms had had a fireplace, but this was going a little bit too far.

I suppose the residence could have been prefabricated if there had been the time, or the interest to think about it, and of course, the money. Practically, however, you only really get to prefabrication when there is repetition on a larger scale. There are elements of prefabrication. The asbestos cement was prefabricated. The formwork was all prefabricated and re-used. In my mind there is really not a great deal of difference in having two or three sets of identical forms that you just move, fill with concrete, let them dry for a couple of days and move again, than assembling pieces in a factory and bringing it out and putting it in place. It makes sense in Russia with its extreme climate and two or three hundred million people but there is a different sort of need here. I am yet to see prefabrication in building take off in Australia. I do not think I will live to see it.

Comment
The disappointments here came about because we were not in charge of the job all the way through. Had we been able to build it ourselves we could have controlled all the details. It would have been a tremendous job.

I can think of a number of things now that I would have done. I could have used the odd tree down those little streets but it is difficult to make changes when you are not involved all the way through. Also, I would have liked to maybe have had a tree or something as the building went back up the hill. That is the sort of thing we could have done had we had been around the job all the time. It would only mean making a few holes in the concrete. It could probably still be done, although if you tried to dig a hole in the concrete now you might find there is a four foot hole filled up with broken glass or some such thing. A building is not really designed until it is finished and changes can easily be made during the course of construction.

The quality of the concrete is poor. It is all patched. There are many, many other things wrong with the building. Built details are crude. Nobody in the College bothered to see whether the contractor was absolutely following the documents or not. It is not really a complicated building at all if you look at it properly. They happened to build it backwards.

As a social environment CCAE is very successful. In this respect it is by far the best of the four residences I have designed. Despite the tight design even the usual problems with noise do not arise. This is a little bit to do with the fact that there are six not 10 in the group. Not all the bed-study rooms open into the living-room but they are all in immediate contact with it. Thus a student can literally put his head out and say, 'Shut up, you bastards'. I think it is the reason there is no noise problem. It was not the architecture, but the programming that was successful. At Guelph six people were the basic unit, and I know that is the right size. What was wrong with Guelph was that we tried to use the lounge to accommodate twelve. This time we said, 'Six is it!' It is a family unit. They can meet others on the street this time. Give them the stoops and the contact close to somebody else's back door, but do not try to more or less artificially or architecturally, or whatever, start and build up these groupings. Socially the CCAE residences are terrific. In detailed building terms, they are a disaster.

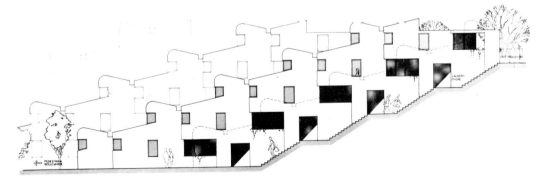

Cross section

Then everything happened again

By 1974 Andrews' Australian practice had expanded and his work was in demand.

In Queensland, further commissions resulted from the combination of the firm's reputation and Simpson's presence. The Chemical Engineering Building for Queensland University and the Australian Environmental Studies Building for Griffith University were designed in Brisbane by Simpson. Co-operation between the Sydney and Brisbane offices was strong and assistance from Sydney helped support the smaller Brisbane office.

The Chemical Engineering Building is interesting because it juxtaposes various design concepts of the firm's earlier work. The Australian Environmental Studies Building complex has affinities with Weldon Library in the immaculate concrete of its load-bearing wall construction. Both buildings are related to their setting in their scale and circulation pattern. Simpson's work is quite identifiable as emanating from the firm, but it is more definitive with tighter compact forms than the expansive planning and generous dimensions typical of Andrews' own designs.

In Sydney, additional staff were employed, and more space obtained by the purchase of the Palm Beach Marine Service, a company which undertakes boat repairs and manufactures marine hydraulic components. The marine services are still run by the firm and continue to operate on the ground floor of the building. The architectural offices are located in the loft. But the life of Australia's building boom was to be limited, and many of the projects remain on the drawing boards.

The design for the Cameron Offices, and the demonstrated ability of the firm to manage successfully schemes of this magnitude, led to its appointment in 1973 as architects for the Woden scheme in Canberra, an even larger government office building for 6000 employees. Though not built as designed, the Woden scheme was not paper architecture. Working drawings were completed and construction was about to commence when the Federal Labor Government's August Budget for 1975 announced a moratorium on most government building programs.

Chemical Engineering Building

Second office at Palm Beach

Australian Environmental Studies Building, Griffith University

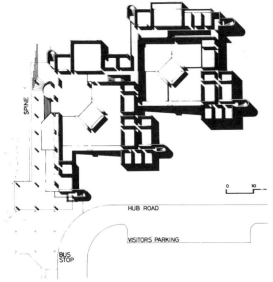

Site plan, Environmental Studies Building

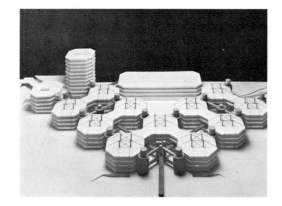

The Woden Offices were to be related to an existing town centre. The site is a 13 acre flood-susceptible plain adjoining the shopping area. In its unused state it presents a barrier between the town and development to the north.

The scheme is made up of three basic functional types – the office spaces, the utility service zones, and the connecting pedestrian movement corridors. The extensive office space requirement is divided into small walk-up garden pavilions, linked by a complex but clearly marked movement network. The intention of Andrews' initial landscape proposal was to avoid channelling the floodwaters, and to allow them to spread delta-like over the site, thus reducing the rate of water movement. This somewhat unconventional and adventurous solution was rejected by the client, and the later scheme provides a channel with one hard edge and one soft edge so that the flood can easily creep. The offices form a viaduct bridging the plain.

The entire complex is elevated above the ground and entered on the second level by a pedestrian path from the existing town centre. Lines of pedestrian and vehicular movement across and on to the site establish the basic net of communication along which the office blocks are grouped, defining open-space courts. The hierarchical differences in the public through-circulation and the private office connections show clearly. The public paths are open, wide, and of sidewalk character, while the more private office connections are enclosed, narrower, and related in character to the carpeted air-conditioned spaces they join. Below the raised building, vehicular traffic is free to move and park. To avoid a dam effect the structure was designed with minimum impediment at its lower level. Four columns located in the central zone of each office pavilion form a compression core from which perimeter pretensioned tension rods suspend the floors. The structural system accommodates heavy loading in the centre, leaving the glass-enclosed external ring open for office use. Wide connections between adjacent modules were planned to permit variation in department sizes on a common level.

Model, Woden Offices

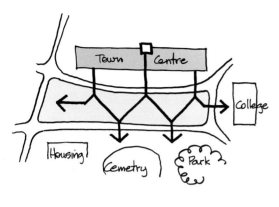

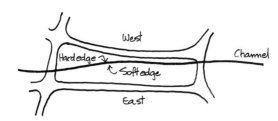

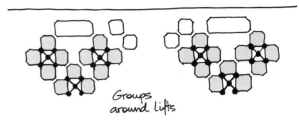

Groups around Lifts

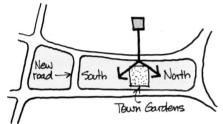

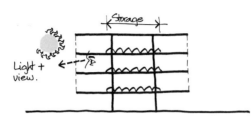

Light + view.

Storage

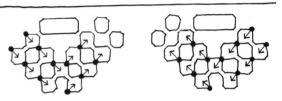

Pedestrians

Parking

Service

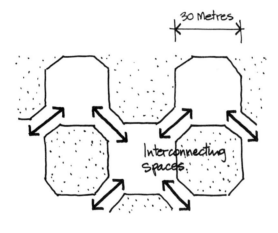

30 Metres

Interconnecting spaces.

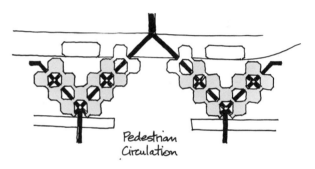

Pedestrian Circulation

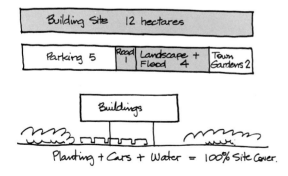

Building Site 12 hectares

| Parking 5 | Road 1 | Landscape + Flood 4 | Town Gardens 2 |

Buildings

Planting + Cars + Water = 100% Site Cover.

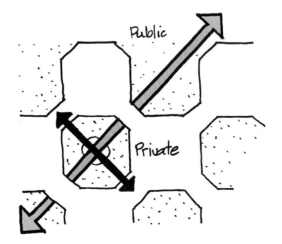

Public

Private

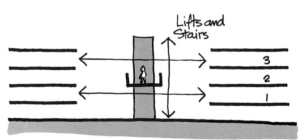

Lifts and Stairs

3
2
1

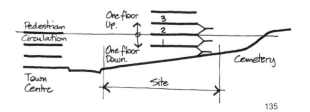

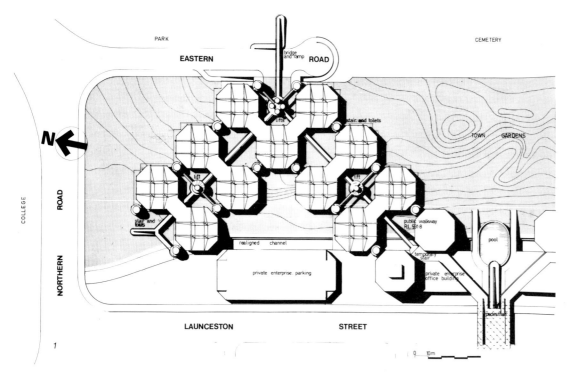

1

1 Roof plan, Woden Offices
2 Model, overview of the Little Bay Housing scheme
3 Model, entry and units of one housing group,
Little Bay Housing
4 Section, Little Bay Housing

2

3

Washrooms, tea-rooms, elevators and stairs are separated from the office units, to allow light into, and views from, these utility zones. The vertical and horizontal movement links are also articulated from the spaces they serve, thus graphically depicting the movement pattern that determined the order of the complex.

The conceptual development of the Woden scheme presents a clear statement of the step-by-step logic of its evolution. Clearly articulated and strictly ordered throughout, the Woden design shows a building system rather than a finite building.

Other work in the office at this time included a low-income housing scheme for the New South Wales Housing Commission. This reveals an extension of the rationale evident in the student housing solutions. As in most countries, the New South Wales Housing Commission became aware that high-rise tower and slab buildings are less than desirable environments for family life. The failure of such solutions led to their search for more socially satisfying, and less visually and climatically disruptive answers with equal economy of site use. The Little Bay scheme for Sydney, presents one alternative.

4

The problem was to provide (at a density of 90 persons per acre) approximately 140 apartments on 3.9 acres of land on a slightly sloping site in a dreary area of non-committal housing, the Long Bay Penitentiary, The Eastern Suburbs Crematorium, Prince Henry Hospital, Bitumen and Oil Refineries, Botany Cemetery, and the Bunnerong Power Station! Over half the apartments were for families. The remainder were single-bedroom units for the aged and for singles and couples without children.

The solution, prepared in the Sydney Office by Doug McKay, branches up the slope, like fingers, from the street. The aged are accommodated at the bottom of the site, nearest the road, where convenience and surveillance are highest. Families are given the central location, and bachelor apartments are placed at the top of the site. Each unit has its own front door entered at ground level from a private covered space for parking and tinkering with cars and bicycles.

Roof-tops and visitor parking covers are also utilized as private open space, while the free land between the fingers provides children's playing areas overlooked by the kitchens in the family units. The fractured forms of the building reflects the variation of spaces within. Construction started in early 1979.

More than a building

The design and construction of the Cameron Offices, which was completed in 1977, spans most of Andrews' time in Australia. Just when confidence in large pedestrian street organized complexes was waning, Andrews came up with this – his clearest statement on that principle. Cameron, quite literally, is a lineal street system which serves the articulated yet related units along its path.

The building, the largest office building in Australia, is a huge complex accommodating 4000 government employees. It was the first building constructed in the town centre of Belconnen – a satellite town outside Canberra ultimately destined to house a resident population of 120 000.

The Cameron Offices were designed around the architect's personal commitment to the deskbound office worker and to the role of the building as a generator of a vital urban order. The major problems posed were: to overcome the inherent sterility and monotony in a scheme of this nature; to provide for the need for individual identity within a structure of such a huge size; to make the complex a positive planning force towards a cohesive urban design; and to accommodate an unpredictable pattern of occupancy by large and small government departments. The success or failure of the scheme will depend on how well it takes its place in the new centre. Nevertheless, even in comparative isolation, it is a remarkable testament to Andrews' design direction.

The 'street', found in embryonic form in his earlier buildings, became in the Australian climate, an elevated open-sided mall to serve as a link, not only between the units of the office complex, but between the elements of the planned housing and commercial infrastructure. The executive suites and function rooms were placed over the mall, and low-rise, walk-up, general office spaces branched off from its spine, creating courtyards between the wings. Full use was made of the sloping site. The spine stepped down to the north, and the office wings down to the west. In this way the complex was reduced to smaller elements that established a rhythm of forms following the contours of the site. The floors of the wings stepped to the north for reasons of access and climatic control. Structural complications that resulted from this were resolved by placing the supporting structures in the courtyard and hanging the office floors between them. The gaunt repetitive forms of the concrete elements are balanced by the play of light on the extensive glazed sections, and the contrast afforded by the planting that interrupts, yet emphasises the stark geometry.

The Cameron Offices, overhead beams of the courtyards

The breakup of the building into the series of low-scaled sections achieved a close association with the landscape by allowing its penetration through the building. The garden courtyards are vast outdoor rooms, overlooked by the building's occupants through the continuous glass walls that line their sides. They are slashed overhead by the gantry beams of the structure, which increase the sense of enclosure. By night they become cavernous spaces defined by the light of the wings that stretch the full depth of the building.

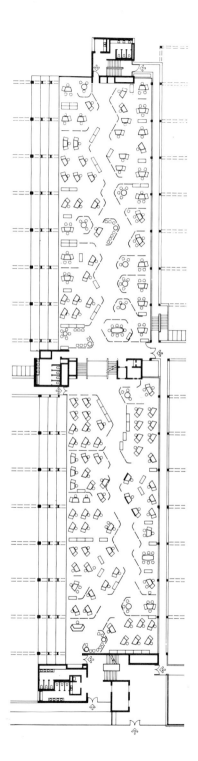

It is a clever solution that intrigues the viewer to seek the clues to its circulation pattern, and to discover the rationale of its 'inside-out' structural system. Once the logic of both is uncovered the design clicks together with remarkable clarity.

The singularity of the arrangement of office accommodation also marks the Cameron Offices as a pioneering structure. For those coming from more conventional buildings the transition was not easy, and initial response to its organization was mixed. Yet more than for any of Andrews' previous buildings, the design for Cameron was concerned with elevating the quality of the work environment.

While the complex is closely integrated and complete within itself, it is clearly a fragment of something much larger. Despite the fact that the interdependence of the parts is one of its major strengths, an extension of the logic of the design would suggest freedom for independent addition. It proposes that a building can, even should, accept a role outside its own program and contribute in a positive way to its setting. But further, Cameron partakes of the benefits of such an integration by bringing diversity into the routine pattern of office activities.

There are obvious affinities between the Cameron Offices and the Woden scheme. Their basic structures, however, follow different architectural directions. Whereas Woden is precise, with channelled paths of movement with distinct relationships to particular parts, Cameron, despite its apparent order, is more of a wandering townscape.

It is not surprising that Andrews considers the Cameron Offices to be his best and most important building. It is of the same calibre as Scarborough, but unlike Scarborough it is a mature building – sophisticated and resolved. While the heavy wall architecture of Scarborough made it a muscular giant, Cameron's columns and beams have produced a bony, but equally commanding companion. The complexities of this building, and there are many, arose from the demanding challenges Andrews set for himself.

Office landscape of one wing

Cameron Offices

The project was a government office complex (now called the Cameron Offices) to accommodate 4000 persons in 600 000 square feet at a cost of $4000 per worker place.

Belconnen, where the project is built, is located behind Black Mountain, 11 miles from the centre of Canberra. The site for the office complex consists of six acres of sheep pasture called Indian Ridge and is between the proposed location of the commercial area and medium density housing. There was only one tree on the site.

The first meeting took place in Canberra in September 1968.

The National Capital Development Commission provided a pre-architectural fee of $5000 to enable us to examine the implications of the site. This examination was begun during this first trip to Canberra, and completed in Toronto. With me in Australia were George Miller, my lawyer, and Richard Strong, a landscape architect with considerable urban design experience, who was obviously going to make a useful input in the planning of the central component of a new town.

Organization

The National Capital Development Commission is the type of operation people look for when time comes to set up an effective government development agency. The NCDC is responsible for the development of the Canberra area and it is autonomous to the end of final design phase, but Cabinet approval is required to enter the next phase, that of construction. The NCDC's annual development budget was $50 million, not large by North American standards, but substantial enough to get a lot of work done over the years.

The organization of the National Capital Development Commission is interesting. There is the Commissioner, two Associate Commissioners (one with the responsibility for finance and the other for construction and development), and the Secretary. Reporting to the Commission are units which cover urban design, planning, architecture, finance, construction, engineering.

The relationships between the NCDC and consultants (called agents in Australia) is straightforward and clear. Everything is contracted out except for urban design and some planning work which is kept in-house. When the consultant gives a major presentation the NCDC members and their unit heads are present. Each unit receives a copy of the proposed solution and analyzes it in terms of its own area of responsibility. Comments are synthesized into a recommendation for the Commission. If the recommendation calls for changes in the proposal the consultant goes back to the drawing-board. If the recommendation is favourable, and the NCDC adopts it, it then goes to the National Capital Planning Committee which is made up of eight or 10 people prominent in the environmental world, including architects, planners, artists, engineers, and two laymen. Approval of this body is followed by presentation to the Cabinet when the project has reached the final design stage.

The result of this type of organization, combined with the calibre of the people, was the absence of the politicking usually found in large projects. As in any organization empires did exist as did those who were busy building or protecting them. At the same time, these people knew their jobs and ran a straight operation. We took our lawyer, George Miller, with us on the first trip to Canberra to discuss the contract and he prepared 11 pages of notes on the NCDC contract which resulted in a new, but good, contract for all parties. The NCDC was as happy as we were. The detailed analysis of the contract by both sides had the effect of ensuring that from the beginning we both understood each other and there was much less possibility of misunderstanding or misinterpretation. If you differed with them it was possible to start a dialogue related to the program involved. There were not the other usual inputs which have nothing to do with architecture.

141

An important ingredient of this relationship was a tight reporting schedule which kept the NCDC informed of our progress and thinking, and which provided them with a decision-making schedule to which they had to adhere in order not to slow the work down. The reporting schedule helped ensure the degree of communication and collaboration between the consultant and client necessary on any project, but especially on large ones. Yet this too had its funny side. The NCDC would decide to hold meetings for the various working parties to discuss the project. Each working party comprised about 20 people. Sir John Overall, the Commissioner, would attend each meeting. The first meeting would begin, presided over by the working party chairman:'Professor Andrews, would you please present the scheme?' I would go through and make a presentation. The first chairman would then get out of the Chair and the chairman of the next working party would preside: 'Now, Professor Andrews, would you please present the scheme?' Then Sir John Overall who had been sitting there each time and had been involved in all the discussions as a member of each committee would then take the Chair: 'Now Professor Andrews would you please present the scheme?' And I would do it for a third time. The same people, maybe an odd one drifted in and out, but there were always about twenty. I presented three times to the same people, in the same room. An extraordinary event that enabled the Commission system to operate yet telescoped the operation to the minimum time available.

Typical of the professionalism of the NCDC operation was the manner in which we were chosen for the project. Overall called from Washington to say that he wanted to drop in and talk to me in Toronto. By the time he arrived we knew who he was, but not what he had in mind or that, as we later discovered, he ran a very tight ship. He spent two days in Toronto behaving like the perfect potential client. He took the office apart, going through it with a fine toothcomb. He read project reports, looked at drawings, examined Metro Centre very closely, talked to Roger du Toit about it and to Bob Anderson about scheduling and

cost control. He spent half a day at Scarborough College looking at it and talking with the Principal and his people about our work. A month later he wrote offering the Belconnen office complex.

The relationship between the architect and the quantity surveyor in Australia is an interesting contrast to that in North America. In North America the quantity surveyor, if he is used at all, has no responsibility. He is usually employed as a cost control consultant to give the architect peace of mind or to add up the builder's sums. In Australia the quantity surveyor is part of the contractual system. He works for the architect, taking off a detailed bill of quantities from the architect's plans. He is responsible for his work and if he is wrong it comes out of his hide. For the Cameron project the Australian quantity surveyor, Don Lawson, came to Toronto for a month during design development and measured every tap and pipe and nail in the drawings.

Four Australian firms were involved in the planning and design of the office complex and principals or owners of all these firms worked with us in Toronto. They were Peter Miller of Miller Milston and Ferris, Don Thomas of D. S. Thomas and Partners, Don Lawson initially of McCredie Richmond and Johns and later of D. R. Lawson Associates, and Peter Courtney of P. J. Courtney Architects. They sat down, rolled up their sleeves and put in a solid month's work. They had talent, years of experience and the authority and willingness to make decisions immediately. It was a delight to work in that way.

Peter Courtney, an old friend in Australia, agreed to become the consulting architect, a requirement of the NCDC if I continued to practise on this project as a Canadian architect. This necessitated Peter leaving his partnership in Canberra and relocating himself at Palm Beach in Sydney, where we jointly decided to establish an office. Two Australians from the Toronto office, Neil Loftus and Graham Walker, also came and Bruce Lincoln who had been with us in Canada agreed to move from Brisbane to Sydney in order to join

us on the project. Two or three local people made up the rest of the team.

At this time I had no partner. I was a sole practitioner. I had had a bellyful of Canadian winters and a few of its other problems and it seemed quite logical that all of those within the firm clamouring to become partners could take over the existing situation in North America, and I would become the partner-in-charge of the Cameron Offices. That entailed a tremendous upheaval, especially the business upheaval of establishing and working in a country under one taxation jurisdiction and drawing money as a salaried employee of a company in another country with another taxation structure. I must admit I very blithely made the decision to move back to Australia with no knowledge of the extraordinary business complications which were to flow out of that decision. I came to Australia for the third series of meetings at the end of 1969, this time to stay.

In retrospect, from many points of view coming back to Australia permanently was an error because once I did not have that plane to catch to return to North America I could not exert the same pressure on the client. I was in Sydney. There was a noticeable difference in attitude once I was not commuting from overseas and I am sure I should have stayed the hell out of here.

A question which absorbed a considerable amount of effort at Scarborough College surfaced again in this project. It was whether or not a lump sum tender was the appropriate method of achieving the required result, financially or architecturally. There had been much discussion about this during the two trips I had made to Australia, I finally received a phone call in Canada telling me that the NCDC had made a definite decision to proceed with the lump sum tender. It was only when I arrived back in Australia that we really began to talk again about the form of contract. By this time we were well into working drawings and had introduced consultants into the process, Peter Miller, the Structural Engineering Consultant, was very much committed to a

Structure in the courtyards

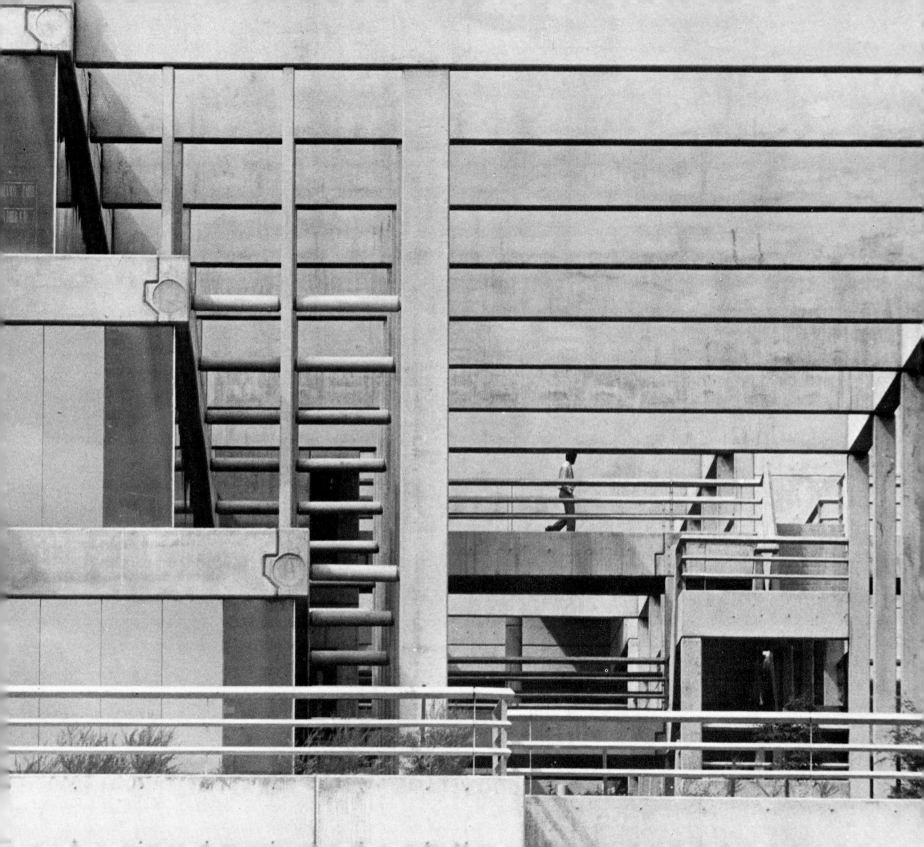

form of contract where the architect and builder could work closely together. Over a period of time the decision for lump sum tender was reversed and we eventually established a contract referred to by the NCDC as a 'co-operative contract', basically one in which the major building contractor is brought into the team earlier than would have been the case on a lump sum tender basis. Under this 'co-operative contract' most of the subcontracts are tendered jointly by the client, the architect and the builder. The process of achieving this was very delicate, as government agencies must maintain public tendering as their major *modus operandi.*

A building of the size of the Cameron Offices cannot be built by just any builder. Many do not have the financial or manpower resources, the experience or personnel with the experience, so there must be some form of selection. It was necessary to advertise in such a way that almost anyone could make a submission, but the terms were clearly enunciated to advise that there was more than money involved in the tender, there was expertise, experience, bank balance and current work load as well. It worked out and T. C. Whittle Pty Ltd were appointed as contractors.

Decisions were able to be made in conjunction with the major contractor before many of the subcontracts had been filled because he was involved almost from the beginning – not as early as I would have liked, but certainly early enough to participate in many of the decisions that gave the building its final form.

Because the building materials were poured and precast concrete it soon became quite obvious that the sensible thing was to produce the concrete on site. Running it around Canberra in trucks was not on; so huge quantities of cement and gravel were stored on the site, and a batching plant established. It also became equally logical to manufacture the precast concrete on site so a precast yard was then set up. The whole idea of precast became quite different once the decision was made to manufacture on site, as

now the builder was always in control and so had considerable flexibility in his operation. For instance, should something happen to the precast work he could readily switch production to poured concrete and work on other parts of the project without having to close the plant down. By incorporating both building techniques into the design, the architect enabled the contractor to balance one part of the construction process against the other. There were many, many troubles but at least we started working with a builder before we as architects had made all of the damn decisions as to where every nut and bolt should go, and how the building was to be built. Architects just are not trained to build or to make builders' decisions.

The NCDC wanted the building completed in three years but nobody knew enough about it to be able to promise this, least of all the builder. The builder did have the opportunity in his tender to say it could not be done in three years, but no tenderer really does that if it means he might miss out on the job. Not one of the tenderers said that it could not be done in that time. They all produced programmes showing how it could be done but, in hindsight, it was obviously an impossible task. I had never done anything as big as Cameron so I had no way of knowing if it was realistic and I doubt if anybody else did, least of all the client. Consequently something which was supposed to be built in three years ended up taking five and maybe a little more.

It took a long time for Tom Whittle to understand the process of this building. He is a very competent, older-type builder. He had no previous experience in building this type of civil engineering project. He had constructed high quality buildings around Sydney but they were one-off, almost handcrafted solutions. This was a very repetitive exercise which meant that quality control of the production line was important, as well as the quality control of the individual craftsmen. Control had to be at a management level as well as a hammer and saw level. It took a couple of years of working together and shouting and screaming and carrying on and writing letters

and threatening law suits backwards and forwards and all sorts of problems before the job began to proceed on an even keel.

There were tremendous problems (design problems according to the builder) with the engineering. For instance every time the builder produced a T-beam it would crack. That seemed horrendous. We finally got down to looking at the crack and found that the engineer was wiping the T-beam with petrol in order to find a crack and, of course, you will find all sorts of cracks if you wipe a T-beam with petrol. The cracks should not have been there anyway, but I think the engineer was being too theoretical. Wrangling over this went on for around 12 months – every beam was rejected as it was made. It was just a dogfight. The specification had deliberately stated that this type of crack should not occur because if people sitting in the building see a cracked beam they think it is going to break. Finally we managed to get some sense out of everybody, and a compromise. I just said I was going to paint the bloody T-beams, which up to that time I had not intended to do. However, by this time I realized that the mechanical engineer would be unable to achieve the new requirement for lighting level if the T-beams were not painted and once T-beams were painted the cracks would be of no consequence as they were not the sort of cracks that would make the building fall down. They saw sense at last. It took a couple of years just to get the builder, the consultants, the client, the people on site and the building itself, all working together. For the last three years, by and large, there was little trouble.

I had an understanding with Tom that if there was a real problem he would give me a call. If I had a real problem, I would call him. If it meant going to Canberra, we would go. If he called me, he paid the fares – if I called him, I paid the fares. That was just a little agreement we had. The first time it happened was at his request – it concerned the T-beams. We met at the airport and went out and solved the problem in an hour or so just by knocking a few heads together and telling people to be sensible. I said to him, 'Well, Tom, you paid the fare, I'll buy the lunch.' So we went into the Bacchus Tavern and we had lunch. This is in the old days when you could have half a dozen oysters and a steak for ten bucks and Tom said, 'I insist on buying the wine. I don't know too much about wine but let's have a bottle.' Anyway, he ordered a wine and the waiter brought it along. It was only two or three years old and Tommy knew enough to say to him, 'Haven't you got anything older than that?' So the bloke brought back a bottle of 1959 Tullochs – a very good red. We had that and a nice lunch and I paid the bill for lunch, which was around 10 or 15 dollars. Tom got the wine bill and it was 23 bucks for that bottle. He nearly died.

The project was an experimental situation for everybody. The client's management was pretty pathetic in some ways. As an example, during the first three years we had something like seven project managers. Project managers are, in the client's terms, relatively sophisticated clerks who are responsible for all the correspondence and red tape. During the same time we had six project architects representing the Commission. It was absolutely bloody chaos. Every time either one of them changed the fellow who took his place had to go back more or less to the beginning and start again. It was only over the last few years of this job that it became relatively steady. We have had one project manager, Fred Cornell, who has been a superb 'clerk' in the sense of keeping everything organized and, with the sort of red tape situation that develops in a project of that size, you need to have someone who is experienced and really knows his way around.

We have also had the one project architect for the last few years. I suppose in many ways he was unnecessary but this depends on how he does his job. If the project architect sees his role as being a sort of spy for the NCDC to make sure you are doing your work, then there are real problems. If he sees his job as being that of helping to minimize the amount of red tape, and as being part of a team to get the job done, he can be a great help. We have experienced both types and even the client

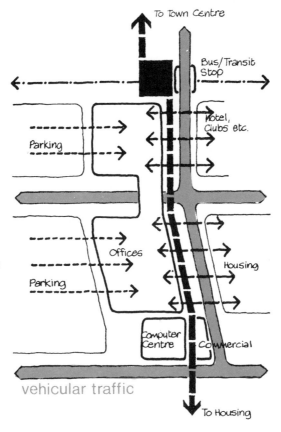

Diagram of the proposed link connections from the Cameron Offices mall

To Town Centre

Bus/Transit Stop

Parking

Hotel, Clubs etc.

Offices

Housing

Parking

Computer Centre

Commercial

vehicular traffic

To Housing

The mall spans the road between the two wings

finally came to realize that if an architect is selected because of his professional capability it is hardly reasonable to install a policeman to watch him.

For the first four years of the administration of the contract Bruce Lincoln moved to Canberra and his place was subsequently taken by Geoff Willing. Between the two of them they administered one of the most complicated and innovative construction procedures undertaken to this day in this country.

The problem
The NCDC's master plan was straightforward. At one extremity of Belconnen lay the major housing area; next to it a merge of housing and commercial; then the main commercial area; the office complex; and, at the top, a lake and public recreation area.

The length of the town site was small and ran only about 2000 feet from end to end. From the office complex area a person could walk through the town centre in less than five minutes, and within 10 minutes be well into the housing area. For these, and other reasons, a totally pedestrian environment was inevitable.

When we first arrived in September 1968 the NCDC was still working on the master plan. The original concept was for a major road running between the office complex site and the town centre which would effectively separate one from the other.

Our argument, subsequently adopted, was that the offices should extend across the major road and create the opportunity, because of the drop in grade, to join the two parts by a pedestrian overpass. This would strengthen the circulation connection between the complex and town centre and provide the basis for a continuous pedestrian route through the town from north to the south.

This discussion about pedestrian environment and road location provided us with the basic determinants of movement, access, convenience, growth, economics and parking, out of which it was possible to extract an

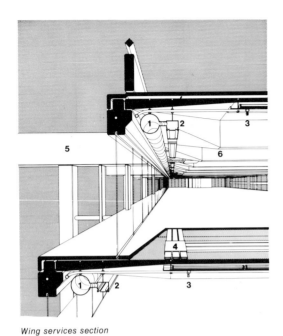

1 Air conditioning duct (exposed)
2 Air outlets (exposed)
3 Combined fire sprinkler and
indirect lighting system (exposed)
4 In-floor electrical and communications system
5 Precast concrete gallows frames
6 Precast concrete T-beams

Wing services section

Structure of the wings showing the tee-beams and gantries

architectural solution. The opportunity was there to design a building as the microcosm of a city. We believed a linear development of this nature and size could easily support one major pedestrian spine, but only one if it was to act as an effective generator of urban life and communal activities. With connected parking facilities, the spine would serve a number of purposes: it would unite and separate office and commercial land uses; it would provide access to these and to services; it would also provide options which could be exercised in the future by plugging in secondary pedestrian routes if the eventual development of the town justified it.

A major factor was the required density: 1 000 000 square feet on six acres gross, 660 workers per acre, the equivalent of a three-storey building covering the entire site. This is downtown density in the middle of a small city. Not even Metropolitan Toronto with a population of 1.8 million reaches that density in the downtown core.

A program requirement was for five 15-storey towers. There was nothing in the NCDC program or the specifications of spaces required which necessitated a high-rise solution. Two things were clear, however. The NCDC specifically wanted to create an urban downtown environment in Belconnen and, in the minds of the NCDC, urbanity meant white towers along the ridge as symbols of the government and the town; the master plan designated towers in the office complex area reinforcing the ridge.

What is urbanity? This was the question over which we battled when I returned to Canberra in December. I argued that urbanity had to do primarily with people, and secondly with the opportunity for people to be in continuous contact with the things which go to make up a city. This does not mean walking across a 500 foot plaza from one building to another. A person walking through a city needs to be involved in a continuing sequence of events whether these be views, buildings, accesses, shops or other people.

The NCDC people argued that this would be achieved through tall buildings. In that sense the attitude of their urban design unit was nineteenth century. New York was their concept of the urban environment and they considered the high towers called for in the master plan would be great to look at. After going round and round at one meeting, we asked the NCDC what their definition or urbanity was, and where they got it from. A NCDC official replied that if we had read Mumford we would know his definition of urbanity and his description of the urbanity of New York. We had read Mumford, and knew that he believed Amsterdam to be more urban than New York.

Urbanity can only be realized in the plane a person walks in or drives through. What is stuck up in the air is of no particular consequence in the creation of an urban environment.

Much of this argument stemmed from the very different ways in which both sides regarded the role of the architect and the responsibility of the client in programming. The NCDC were accustomed to architects operating on a largely intuitive basis, who walked into a presentation with drawings the client either had to approve or reject. That is easy for the client. Nine times out of 10 the presentation will be approved because, having hired the well-known architect to do the job, to contradict him is like the client stomping on his own toes.

The NCDC were unaccustomed to being involved in an on-going dialogue with the architect and sitting down with him to probe problems. That required much more involvement and much more trouble than they had expected.

This approach, as opposed to the intuitive one, is, of course, hell for the architect as every thought and every idea is exposed and available for comment and there are no secrets and no surprises. I often envy the architect who can convince himself that total intuition is the way to go.

The second source of argument at that December session was our preliminary design concept. There had to be space for a building and space for parking. It seemed reasonable to park all over the site and build on top of the parking. Workers could then drive to a position under their offices, park, and walk up to their desks, eliminating the cars from view and maximizing access. Politically this was not on, whatever the concept's intrinsic merits. We were proposing covered parking for civil servants when Members of Parliament did not have it. I was a bit bloody uptight about the concept. We had the land available. There was no point in wasting it in a sprawl, but there was also no point in imitating a downtown development by stuffing as much as possible into the smallest possible area. Overall said, 'No. No covered parking.' We took a hell of a beating for the first week.

The last meeting of the week was a total disaster at the end of which everybody looked at each other and said, 'Where do we go from here?' I said I was going to Palm Beach for the weekend and would let them know on Monday whether or not we would continue with the project. Some of my people wanted to stand on principle and refuse to alter the concept simply to appease some Members of Parliament who might be annoyed if civil servants got covered parking before they did. I was not interested in creating a situation in which we did not build because of a questionable principle. So we went back to the drawing-board and looked at the problem again. The result was something much better than the first concept; a viable, highly flexible system of office space tied to an urban pedestrian environment.

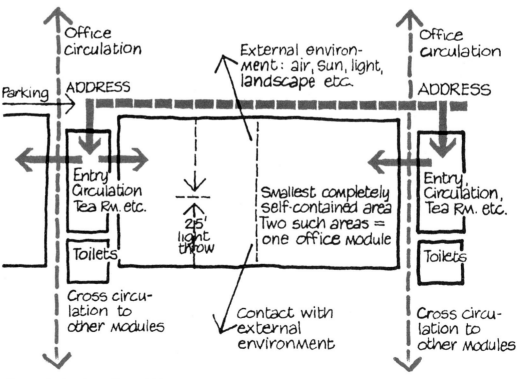

Diagramatic plan of one office module

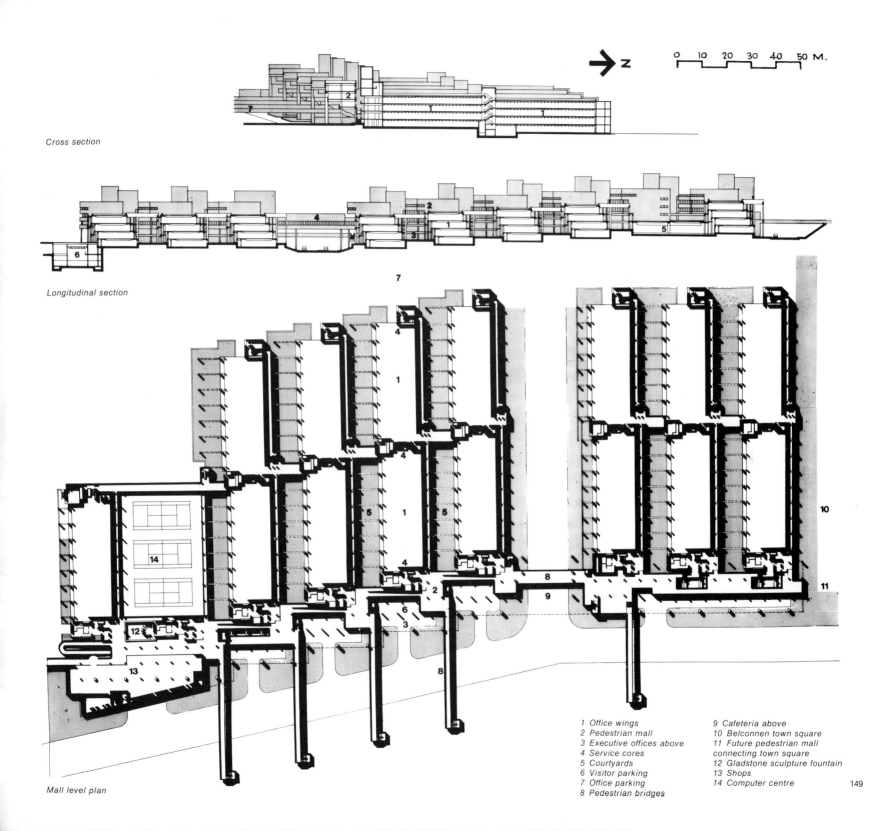

Cross section

Longitudinal section

Mall level plan

1 Office wings
2 Pedestrian mall
3 Executive offices above
4 Service cores
5 Courtyards
6 Visitor parking
7 Office parking
8 Pedestrian bridges

9 Cafeteria above
10 Belconnen town square
11 Future pedestrian mall
connecting town square
12 Gladstone sculpture fountain
13 Shops
14 Computer centre

149

Connecting levels in the mall

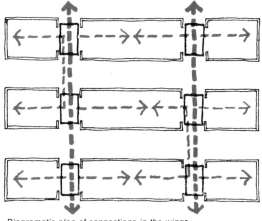

Diagramatic plan of connections in the wings

The big thing on Belconnen was to get from the Government through the NCDC a 'Notice to Proceed' to the builder. So we planned a 'Notice to Proceed' party with a band and the works at my house. That time was terribly tense because during these months there were times when they were going to do it, and times when they were not going to do it. We had these 'Notice to Proceed' invitations, specially designed by Gordon Andrews all ready, although we had to change the date on them about four times! A hundred or more people came to the house and it was interesting. The pressure had built up and built up. People came from the NCDC, the builder and the consultants. There were many tensions released at that 'Notice to Proceed' party. Mortal enemies came to understand each other and to realize that above personal positions there was a building at stake.

The solution
The solution is a system of flexible office spaces providing one million square feet to accommodate government departments which grow and change from month to month and year to year. The first tenant was to be the Bureau of Statistics. However, in five or ten years there may be 25 different departments and agencies there.

Cameron is a staged development, as anything as big as that has to be. The first stage to be completed was the computer for the Australian Bureau of Statistics which contains pretty well everything about everyone in the country on a reel or a card. That had to be available as quickly as possible. It has now been in operation since 1975. The computer had to be housed in a vast, flat plate of one-storey. Its roof, at pedestrian concourse level, is admirably suited to tennis courts as part of a social entertainment unit.

As each wing was finished, or a group of wings, the departments moved in and occupied. In 1975 there were three different departments in occupancy. The whole building was intended eventually for the Australian Bureau of Statistics, but who knows what may happen and it does not really matter. The

complex was designed to take one great big department, any combination of other large departments or a multitude of small departments.

The building is a half-landing, walk up grid three to four and a half storeys in height. Each floor consists of eight thousand feet, half a level above and half a level below the adjacent floors. All the floors are joined by ramps to allow the mailboy with his cart to go anywhere without having to face stairs. Each module is potentially self-contained with its own toilets, tea room and entrance from the outside connecting to an inter-office circulation system.

From a point mid-way in the grid three times as much floor space is accessible in a 45 second walk as would be in a conventional slab tower with 15000 square feet per floor.

Running from north to south of the office site is a 31 foot drop in grade. This provided the means for establishing an elevated pedestrian mall crossing the major intersecting road and connecting the offices to the town centre to the north. The office complex sits like seven fingers poking off the mall courtyards. Each wing has an elevated sidewalk to allow direct entrance from the outside into the individual modules and an entrance at the back of the building from the carpark for rear circulation. Like Complex B at Guelph, the system can be treated as one building, 14 separate buildings, or any number in between.

Maximum opportunity for address points for the public was important. An office system which requires walking through one department to reach another is unsatisfactory, so is one which does not allow each department and office to have a public address point.

The system had to allow a department to grow without having to divide itself into physically separate sections distant from each other or forcing neighbouring departments back into corners of buildings without a direct address to the outside circulation system. Consequently,

Restaurant on the mall

there are address points off the car level, off the major pedestrian spine, and the back streets. These address points ensure that each wing, on each floor, can actually afford to contain four little tiny units each with its own publicly accessible front door.

Between adjacent office fingers are a series of courtyards, each one with its own distinctive ecological character. In this way the immediate view for the 50 foot wide offices is entirely different from one side to the other, and it is the landscape that provides the knowledge as to where you are in the complex rather than the architecture. The courtyards, as they were finally detailed, vary from a hot-dry desert situation through the spectrum of Australian landscape to that of a swiftly running mountain stream (complete with fish). As a final touch of class the graphics and furnishings were co-ordinated with the landscape, ranging from hot-warm colours in the desert area to cold-cool colours in the mountain stream location.

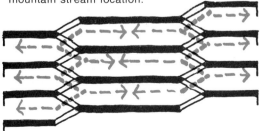

Diagramatic section of half-level connections within each wing

The courtyards are filled with greenery and water, the roofs covered with ground cover so that the residents in the nearby buildings will not have to look down on gravel and asphalt roofs. The roof recreates the open space supplanted by the building. Staff lunch rooms are up there, opening out into this introduced landscaping. No point in any module is more than 25 feet from the outside and a level and one-half from greenery. The planting in the courtyards is very visible to everybody. It is there if you want to walk anywhere near a window and it is certainly evident from all the walkways.

A neighbourhood shopping centre is available within the complex for the occupants and inhabitants of a planned housing group just across the road. Above the bridge over the road there is a restaurant serving the complex.

The climate in Canberra is extreme for Australia. Occasionally during the winter the nights are cold enough to create a thin layer of ice on a pond, but the days are warm even during the winter and during the summer they are damned hot. The buildings had to respond to this climate so the interior spaces are air-conditioned. The variety of shading and cooling devices around and over the building eliminates direct sunlight from the windows thus allowing each module to be treated as one zone of air-conditioning, with no perimeter zones and creates efficiencies and economies of operation.

Within the modules it was essential to provide as much open space as possible, uncluttered by structure and service ducts. As the building was relatively low and multiple floors were not involved it seemed possible to use one floor to shade the one below. The spine was very obviously going to run east and west so the wings faced due south. We also needed identical floor sizes as the building was to be so big it became pretty clear that mass production of floor elements would be a sensible thing. We were also looking for free spans to avoid columns going up through the middle of office spaces.

The building steps out so that the pedestrian mall and elevated footpaths can be tucked in out of the sun and open to the breeze much like the traditional Australian verandah. The stepping action of the building made an interior column solution difficult and wasteful.

The solution was to take the columns outside the buildings and use the courtyards for structure. The interior spaces are then uninterrupted, fifty-two foot spans sitting between courtyards which incorporate the structure frames with the weight of one building balancing the weight of the adjacent. As always, the best way to solve a problem is to eliminate it.

This is a very simple answer to these problems as it allows all of those things to happen. It is a miraculous solution from the point of view of economy of structure as there would not be one inch of concrete or one pound of steel that was unnecessary.

The sun comes from the north so by pushing the whole thing over the sun can penetrate into the courtyard down the sloped side. Even the gallows beams actually shield the very low western summer sun off the south facing glass. There are a couple of places on the top floor where the sun penetrates. In fact, what happened is that there was to be one piece of concrete acting as a sunshade but it was taken away in the mad rush to cut costs. It is the only place in that whole building that the architecture does not work as a sunshade. The Australian Bureau of Statistics lived in the Treasury Building. There they occupied large areas with vinyl tile floors and breakfast-food ceilings, hundreds of desks and occasional half height glass boxes with supervisors in them. The people sitting at the desks literally had green eye shades and they needed them. There was floor after floor of these people.

We simply set out to make a better environment for large numbers of people who worked together in one area at desks or punch card machines. The executives had, and still have, their places to go for privacy. These are located above the pedestrian mall.

The main problem with the office landscaping is that the occupants just got carried away. With outdoor landscaping so apparent from all parts of the building, indoor potted plants everywhere are unnecessary. A couple of the wings look like indoor plant nurseries complete with Norfolk Island pines growing in tubs. I am not going to be responsible when they reach the ceiling, that is for sure.

Although parts of the Cameron Offices have been occupied since 1975, the complex was not totally occupied until 1977 and has yet to take its place as part of the overall urban fabric of Belconnen Town Centre. The connections to medium density housing and bus terminal are still under construction with the commercial facilities only partially tenanted.

When they finished the thing the NCDC put on *their* show. They had tea and biscuits. That was really something. After eight years bloody tea and biscuits. Hundreds and thousands and

Walkways to the bus station

green icing stuck on little biscuits. In anticipation of this we had arranged for a gathering of the people who had been actually involved over the eight years and roasted a pig and sheep. Even so to creep away to your own party after one-fifth of your actual life devoted to one building could only be called a bit of an anti-climax.

Comment
My criticisms would be more a feeling of intense disappointment and frustration that the NCDC was unable to control the external pressures that changed the planning organization of the town centre, and moved the shopping centre from its place within the overall design system at a time when the Cameron Offices were almost completed. We have been able to remedy this situation partially by connecting the mall to the bus station, and thence in a very tenuous way to the new location of the shopping centre. It is impossible to assess to what extent this replanning will affect the fundamental premise of the organization of the Cameron Offices.

The Cameron Offices from the west

Low energy
let down

1976 and 1977 marked recession years for building in Australia. Private enterprise reacted first with the cancellation of commercial work. With the stoppage of government building, architectural offices engaged primarily on large-scale projects found themselves with little, if any, ongoing work. The Andrews' office was badly hit with the cancellation of all projects, with the exception of those in Queensland. The entire Sydney staff moved into the Marine Services building and the original office was leased for other uses.

Cuts in government expenditure meant that little hope remained for the implementation of the plan for the town of Monarto, a new growth centre for Adelaide, the capital of South Australia. Situated 40 miles from the city in an arid, semi-desert environment, Monarto's single virtue was its location on the main water pipeline to the interior. Andrews was commissioned in 1975 to prepare the urban design for the new town centre and to co-ordinate the work of a six-architect team invited to design specific projects within the scheme. This provided the first opportunity to create the integrated urban mix that the Cameron Offices could only suggest.

The covered mall became a varied open pedestrian street connecting the transportation terminal and a symbolic and functional energy tower to the north-west, with the artificial lakefront to the south-east. Mixed along this pedestrian spine were schools and colleges, shops and offices with housing on their upper floors, and small-scale recreational facilities. Access roads, service drives and parking places were restricted to the perimeter of the pedestrian area. Offices shared the lakefront with housing, sporting facilities, and the hotel. An urban pedestrian waterfront plaza connected with the science centre related to the conserved marshlands, and led around to the minor pedestrian paths that skirt the lakeside.

The Monarto proposal provides an example of a low energy development for a hot, dry climate. Buildings were located and designed to utilize prevailing winds for cooling. Construction materials varied depending on position (horizontally and vertically), building use, and patterns of occupancy, in order to derive the maximum potential environmental benefit. Solar energy collectors were integral features of the building

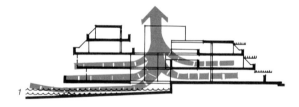

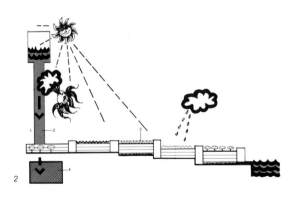

1 Monarto, diagram showing the movement of cooled air current through the buildings
2 Cooling and heating energy ring
3 Monarto town plan

1 Water tower
2 Transportation terminal
3 Retail
4 Police, Fire, Ambulance
5 Performing arts centre
6 Health and welfare
7 Church precinct
8 Offices
9 City centre housing
10 Applied arts
11 Technological studies
12 Environmental studies
13 Business & General studies
14 Schools administration

15 Library resource
16 Primary school
17 Science centre (schools)
18 Secondary school
19 Pre-school
20 Indoor sports centre
21 Hotel
22 MDC offices
23 Science centre
24 Lakeside housing
25 SHort term parking
26 Long term parking
27 Service station

design. The most imaginative exploitation of low-energy sources came through the use of water. As the lake had to be maintained artificially from the pipeline, it was proposed to service the length·of the mall with a mini-train service powered by the energy generated from the fall of water from the tower. The fall provided the pressure for the path of water that flowed down beside the mall and under the adjacent structures. The office blocks were designed around water courts, through which the water passed on its way to the lake. The detailed design reinforced the evaporative cooling system by exploiting the psychological effects of the sight and sound of the moving sheets of water.

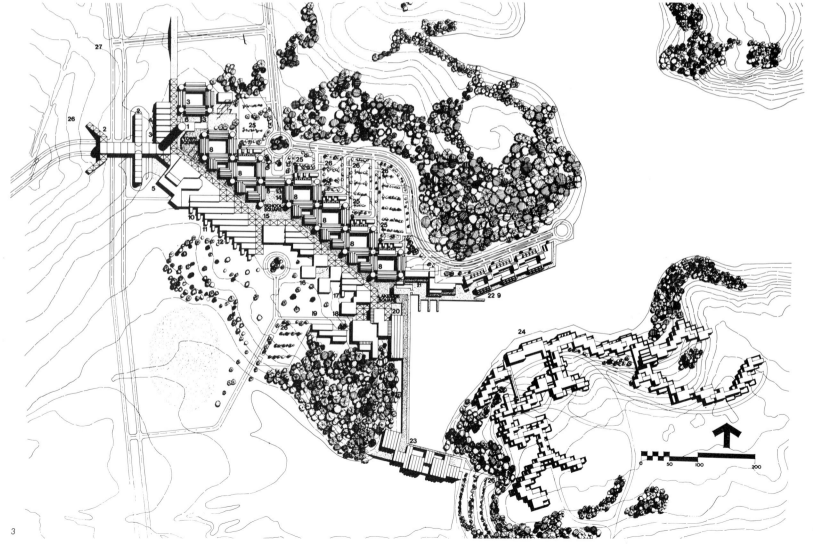

3

1

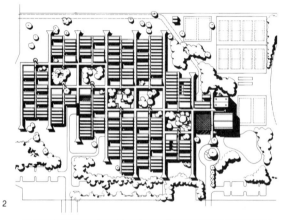

2

3

High in density, yet low in profile and energy consumption, and with its intended mixture of activities, the Monarto plan held high promise as a viable social and physical environment.

Close collaboration between Andrews and the mechanical engineer Don Thomas, has resulted in progressive energy saving solutions that respond to the fluctuating temperature changes of Australia. Air-conditioning and heating systems have been simplified by the building designs that avoid the big load swings of both summer and winter conditions. Thomas has integrated combinations of tried and proven results from industry to produce waste heat recovery systems which have eliminated the need for boilers and cooling towers, even in the extreme climate of Canberra.

Ideas for recycling waste and utilizing low energy systems were, in part, accepted by the clients for the Cameron Offices. The design for a high school in Perth shows a quite ingenious system for evaporative cooling that is both a service and an architectural feature. The school will not be built – clients are nervous of unconventional answers.

Three modified modules of the Woden scheme, for use as a technical college (with expected future additions for other uses), were constructed in 1979. In this scheme, heat is recovered from the refrigeration plant, laboratory discharges, and general space use, for storage in large water tanks adequate to accommodate all winter loading fluctuations. The tanks will also store heat from solar collectors (integral parts of the original design) once (if) they are installed. With a progressively minded client for Monarto, the South Australian Government, the possibility for the creation of a total low-energy town became very real.

At the beginning of 1978 the Australian building industry remained at a low ebb, but there were some signs of a lifting of restraints. Construction had commenced on the Lecture Theatre and Staff Offices for the Darling Downs Institute of Advanced Education and the Kelvin Grove College of Advanced Education Library, Brisbane, and a start was planned on the Library and Student Union Building for the Royal Melbourne Institute of Technology.

The Kelvin Grove Library relates to the previously prepared planning scheme for the College. It is a strongly modelled concrete building that ties existing structures together and with them defines a restful landscaped court.

4

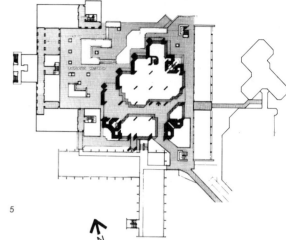

5

1 Woden College of Technical and Further Education;
under construction
2 Mandura High School, Perth
3 Educational Resources Centre, Kelvin Grove College of
Advanced Education
4 Lecture theatre and staff offices building, Darling Downes
Institute of Advanced Education; east elevation
5 Site plan, Education Resources Centre

Forming up and filling in

The RMIT Library and Union was designed for an urban location in the midst of the haphazard development of the area of the Institute in the inner city. This is an infill building to stand on the site of a previously demolished structure. As on so many earlier occasions the building assumes a major role in connecting the existing pedestrian circulation systems. In this instance the building, which is restrained on all sides, is split into two sections allowing a public path to pass through. Movement from one section to the other passes over elevated glass-enclosed bridges that span the open path. The angling of the structure 45 degrees to the boundaries creates pockets of space between the new building and those adjoining. Secondary functions and services are located in the central and side open spaces, freeing the major structure from interruptions. The full resolution of the purity and simplicity of the waffle slab and column system with glass-block walls is the outstanding characteristic shown in the design of this building.

Andrews' knack of turning constraints and hindrances to advantages is particularly evident here. It seems that the greater the obstacle, the more he enjoys the combat and the more resolved the outcome.

Royal Melbourne Institute of Technology Library and Student Union

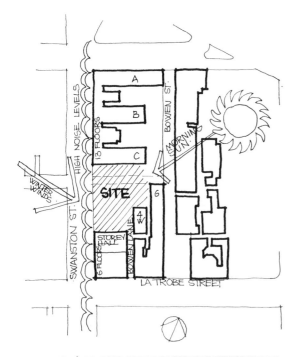

The site, Royal Melbourne Institute of Technology Student Union and Library

The job at Royal Melbourne Institute of Technology to design a Student Union/ Library facility came from our performance in Australia. By this time the overseas content of expertise for convincing clients was becoming less necessary and less useful, as buildings such as the Cameron Offices, King George Tower and Chemical Engineering at Queensland University were completed and had established their own reputations. The overseas influence only became involved because Evan Walker had been in Canada and knew my work there, and we had continued to have contact when each of us came back to Australia. He was in a responsible position as Vice President of RMIT, so that must be how we got to be on a long list for an institution in Melbourne, a city which traditionally does not go too far looking for architects.

The long list is a procedure which is pretty common in North America but was rare in Australia. The routine is: the long list, the interviews, the presentation, the short list, the re-interview, the re-presentation, then, finally, the appointment. This is very much a North American way to do things, part of the performance. That is part of the art – part of the performing art, being able to handle those situations and size up the people in them and react to them instantaneously. If you are wrong you do not get the job. You almost have to know how to dress for the occasion – getting the job is the important thing – keeping your personal views on fashion for another time.

The whole redevelopment of RMIT had been allocated beforehand, and a large part of it had already been built by a long established architectural firm in Melbourne, not in my favourite way. In this case the client, when they finally got their $15 or $20 million worth of work so far, found they really did not want it. They did not think it worked; they did not think it looked good. So they decided to try somebody else.

There was some adverse reaction amongst Melbourne architects when we got the job. They seemed to believe that in this day and age work should go to locals. I cannot believe

in that attitude. In a time of economic downturn when there is very little work, the clients are going to be able to spend more time looking and will even look for higher quality and, consequently, further afield than they might in boom times.

The problem

I find no particular disadvantage in doing a job in Melbourne from Sydney. In fact, this has been the pattern of our practice for years. We had our office in Toronto but have done only one building and a renovation to an old house for an art gallery there. The firm has always been what is described by the A.I.A. as a 'core firm' keeping the numbers limited and being able to respond to the need to build wherever the job may be, not proliferating offices as 'branches' but doing the work at the central place and locating a site office with the sole responsibility of building the particular project. The branch office situation breeds only mediocrity and division.

In this case we were asked to renovate an existing building of the recent development which is, for want of a better description, an office type; to upgrade the library space that already existed within it; and to build some student union facilities on an adjoining site. In looking at the problem we found that it had been stated exactly backwards. We could get more student union facilities and accommodate them better within the lower levels of the existing building, plus a section in the new building, because student facilities need to be where people are.

You could spend all the money you wanted, and do all the renovation you wanted, but you could never justify the library needs in the existing structure because the form of building was wrong, it had the wrong column spacing, the wrong aspect, the wrong organization. You could gussie it up, but it would never work. The Library needed to be the new building. That proposal was presented and approved. In fact we turned the whole brief around. Instead of renovating the existing Library we proposed building a new Library incorporating, in its lower levels, student facilities, and redesigning the lower levels of the existing facilities for student use. In that way the Student Union would be a continuous succession of activities at ground level, consistently accessible to the movement paths of pedestrians.

The upper levels of the existing building would be for academic expansion – another part of the problem. It was originally designed for academic space anyway, offices, classrooms and those sorts of small specific spaces that do not have lots of people going to them. It operated on an elevator system with the Library about two floors above the ground. Within certain periods some 2000 people want to use the Library and elevators just do not handle that sort of access at all well. A library needs to be entered from ground level where it is constantly and conveniently available, not hidden away at the end of a journey by elevator.

Due to bureaucratic upheavals funding for the project as originally designed was cut off as we were about to proceed into contract documentation. The project was revised in late 1978 in a reduced form, the first stage being Union facilities of a more modest nature. It now looks as though the Library will go ahead within the next three years before the Union finishes construction.

This time we are working with a totally new amount of money, a new organization, and a new set of controls. A lot of parameters, particularly the physical parameters of the structure on the site, remain precisely the same. The new building, at a quick glance, is a very close relative of the old one, the major difference being that it is now a two, or even three, stage operation instead of a one stage operation.

There are more students at RMIT than there are soldiers in the Australian Army, and they exist on six acres in the city in a relatively low-rise type of development. It is the biggest tertiary educational institution in the Southern Hemisphere. It has full time, part time, night time courses; people learn there in all sorts of ways.

RMIT is a very old campus. It is right in downtown Melbourne. It is a dream situation in that it has a main station for the new subway under construction about 50 yards from the campus. All around are places to eat and places to go. You can easily walk to the city centre. It is one of the classic positions for any campus.

A lot of the buildings there are reasonable structures. In the 'golden times' with money everywhere people thought, 'Oh! Bloody old thing. Why don't we pull it down and build a new one?' That had been the attitude of the previous master plan, but it is no longer appropriate in today's terms when money is short. So the bulldozer plan that had been proceeded with has been stopped short and replaced by a new attitude towards development, an attitude now much more interested in refurbishing as opposed to total rebuilding, but which has left us with a site between the new development of Casey Wing and the old Storey Hall.

The significance of RMIT to me is the opportunity to look at the problem of infill and rejuvenation; to take a dense active urban campus and sensibly organize the pedestrian movement in a convenient way without overdoing the bulldozer technique; to develop new accommodation and new spaces within the existing framework. It is the reverse of most things I have had to do before. They have all been surrounded by at least a moose pasture, or been able to exist on their own – jewels if you like. Now this one is quite the reverse. You almost never see it except when you are in it, surrounded as it is on three sides by existing buildings and with a noisy street on the fourth side.

Perspective from Swanson Street

The solution

At the moment there is no apparent organization, no system of movement through the campus. This was an obvious opportunity to pull the whole thing together. It puts the library at the heart of the campus, it puts the major student facilities at the heart of the campus, and it pulls all the ground level pedestrian circulation together into the one system, maximizing the opportunity for convenience and contact. That is an old story for me. It is still what it is all about regardless of whether it is infill or jewel; whether it is in Melbourne or Toronto. It is still the major genesis of any building.

The building itself sits in between Swanston Street, a part of a circulation pattern of RMIT, and Bowen Street, a private roadway acting as the central spine of RMIT. The change in level between those two streets is about two storeys. Half-way between those streets through the old building system is another circulation path called Bowen Lane. Our new building straddles, and forms the transition of, all of these pedestrian movement systems.

Bowen Street runs up and down the middle of the campus. The building opens up a space off Bowen Street and brings people into a position where they can have access to the Bowen Street circulation level of the already existing buildings. It picks up Bowen Lane, it picks up Swanston Street and it brings them, one way or another, to the same point.

The original development scheme planned to put a new building on Bowen Street between Casey and Gillespie Wings, but the demolition of the old building made it apparent that this area was better left as an open space in the middle of the campus. We have reinforced the significance of this space by our concentration of all the pedestrian circulation at that point.

A serious consideration of the new design had to be allowing construction access for the second stage. Part of the site is unused in the first stage which allows the remaining undemolished building to be useful, and when the Library comes along that building (4 West)

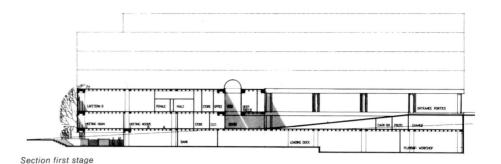

Section first stage

Level 4 plan

will be removed. In order to remove the building access has to be available and this is only possible off Swanston Street. Bowen Lane is too narrow to take that sort of traffic, so the space between the Union and Storey Hall is absolutely critical to allow for building in the future – both from a demolition and a construction point of view.

The new building will be seven storeys; the existing Casey Wing is twelve. There is not much you can do about that except to be gentle with the module, an expressed vertical column module. On the opposite side is a blank brick wall with a neo-something-or-other facade where height and proportion are the essence. Known as Storey Hall the building

has an historical classification and is to be retained as a permanent part of the street facade. Our building accepts this height, and sets itself back so that the rectangular form of Storey Hall can sit and be itself.

The major dining and lounge facilities for the Union are on the Bowen Street level, the main level throughout the campus. They are on the Swanston Street side where they have light and view. The level below the dining facilities is first of all the Union offices which face Swanston Street where they also have light and view, and behind them are the billiard room, typing area, gymnasium and some of the lounges. The level below that is the Swanston Street frontage.

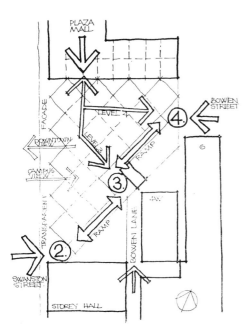

Diagram of internal circulation

The Federal funding now involved is very precise and strict in terms of what can be built with the funds they provide. They will not finance squash courts and things of that nature but they will pay, for instance, for a theatre – so there is a theatre at the Swanston Street level. The theatre can be used at night without traipsing through the rest of the campus and it has an address point in Swanston Street, which is the ideal place for it. There are other public facilities there – facilites which not only have to do with the campus but also with the public.

One minor little bit of a breakthrough was the bank on the Swanston Street level which has to be paid for separately. A bank with the opportunity for a captive audience of 25 000 students will pay a lot of money, from which can come some of the funding for the Union building, maybe allowing us to go a little bit beyond the budget allowed by the Federal Government.

Servicing can occur off the existing underground truck tunnel with a loading dock and vertical distribution.

The second stage will provide 9290 m² (100 000 square feet) of library space. A library has a couple of specific requirements, not many. There is an obvious environmental quality to it, it must be a comfortable place to be in. It needs to be capable of constant rearrangement and reorganization collectionwise, how you see from librarian to librarian, how you supervise.

The structural system is dictated by the Library as it is the major component of the total project. The other elements in the building are not things that have in themselves a precise structural need.

The building next door is based on a 6.706 m (22 foot) module which is too small to continue in the Library. It needed to be a 9.45 m (30 foot) span or thereabouts, so simply by taking off at 45 degrees to the existing grid, it always touches the grid at exterior column points – very well mannered. It touches precisely and I get 9.48 m (31 feet 1½ inches), near enough all things considered. This solution allows light for the new Library and the existing buildings on all sides via triangular light shafts so formed between the new and old buildings. There is obviously no view, but a strong need for natural light which we have provided with translucent glass-block walls. We are not really concerned with being able to look out from this building except in the middle where it has been torn apart for half a module for the major pedestrian connection from one level of the campus down to the street.

The interior walls are clear glass and the carrel seating overlooks the pedestrian path. Coming up through the building, you are going through it and aware of all its levels.

You can imagine the librarians' reaction to having a nice square box and then having it pulled apart. They nearly had a fit. We pointed out that bookshelves are arranged between access corridors, and however these are

Model

161

located, the flexibility of arrangement of the bookshelves is not lost if the circulation corridor becomes a little glass bridge for 4.572 m or 6.096 m (15 to 20 feet) instead of being lined by rows of bookshelves. It does not interfere with the working of the place at all. They were pretty hard to convince, being concerned only about the ultimate theory of library planning, but were finally convinced of the importance of the 'break' to the total campus plan.

By pulling the new building apart and having a succession of three staggered bridges of three floors, the movement of people crossing from one part of the Library to the other can be seen from pedestrian ramps below. At the same time a presence of the rest of the campus can be provided by the slot from the Library much better than by a sign or even a knowledge of where it is. It is like the Humanities Wing at Scarborough College. There is a visual integration. It does not affect the workings of the building at all but you can see it all happening. This becomes even more important when, due to the proximity of other buildings and the problem with western sun, the exterior skin lets in light but does not afford an outlook.

The basic open plan of a library is straightforward but elements having impact like stairs or elevators or toilets or air-conditioning must be completely organized. If you are going to have a free organizable, rearrangeable type space, you do not want a duct down through the middle of it. So, really what we have provided is a very simple frame turned at an angle which touches its surroundings as opposed to paralleling its wall with their wall. The structural column and slab have been kept absolutely pure without penetration. It is reminiscent of Kahn in that it has servant spaces and served spaces but there is not a penetration through a slab anywhere, or a wall for that matter. Every system is very clearly articulated and in its own place.

Where there is a partition it is an incidental element, like for a typing room or a library. In such cases you obviously have to take the partition to the ceiling because of a need to be soundproof, but they are the 'odd men out' so you might as well take the advantage of the economy of no ceilings. Once we could see the purity of the things emerging it became even nicer to take all of these attendant elements such as stairs, elevators and toilets and locate them in such a way that the frame was untrammelled. That gives an interesting result from a construction point of view.

As the Library is not being fully designed just now it may need to be a bit bigger than was planned before, but as the only possibility is to build over the top of the Union, which will shortly start construction, the decision has to be made now in terms of numbers of floors, so columns and footings can be put in. We are talking of an extension of the structural system with a different floor loading.

We hope that the construction of the Library will start before the construction of the Union is finished otherwise you have that silly nonsense of a temporary roof on the Union which could maybe be there for a very short period of time but is a big cost. It makes common sense to follow one behind the other if possible.

The pedestrian ramp through the slot in the completed building forms is a construction joint between Stage 1 and Stage 2. The Union is totally on one side, and the Library on the other, but coming across the top of the Union.

The space goes all the way through the building – it has to have the sky above, as it is a building totally pulled apart. Natural light is essential otherwise it would be just a long, depressing tunnel. Along the footpath rain can fall on you. We have provided, at the footpath level, places where you can get out of the rain and look in a shop window, places where you can take that momentary pause. You can come in and up the first part of the ramp, enter the building and go on your way, all the way through most of the campus without going out in the rain. If you wish you can go further up and about the campus in a more exterior way.

RMIT currently has no sense of identity, no sense of arrival. There is an opportunity here to have a front door right on Swanston Street. It is the logical place for a front door as it is on a tram-line; it is a place to stop; it needs to receive people and get them into the campus. The Union facilities are quite distinct and separate from the Library but they both have a major entrance at the principal people level off Bowen Street. At present, the students do not use the Library to the degree they should, because, being hidden on upper floors, it has no presence whatsoever. The new Library will have its own identity, yet it is not a precious separate structure like most libraries. It is not a monument to books. It is a very intrinsic and involved part of the campus yet is remote enough in its vertical separation not to be unworkable because of noise. It is right there, bang in the heart of the campus. You can go downstairs and get a cup of coffee or hamburger in the bistro or whatever, or play ping-pong, simply by taking an elevator or a stair. You can go back up and read if you want. This Library should be very well used just because of where it is and what it is.

This building, probably as much as any, is very much related to the title of this book – architecture being a performing art. The performance here had to be a very theatrical one to start with and the actual performance as far as we are concerned has had to be far beyond what you are normally being paid for. Then there has been the performance of endurance, of just sitting with it and staying with it, but out of all that it seems to me that RMIT are getting their problem solved. I am rather glad in a way that they did not build what we originally designed, because the later design is better than the first, and it is better because the whole process has become more refined and the need for theatrics is less than it was in the first place.

Culture and climate

In the late seventies Andrews produced some of his most interesting work despite the depressed state of the building industry in Australia. Included was a series of schemes for houses for his family, and the Intelsat Headquarters design.

Determined to keep his staff and himself involved and active despite the 1975 recession, Andrews commenced a design of a house for his family at Palm Beach. While this exercise was primarily a creative outlet, it served as exploratory ground for many ideas for denoting ways to develop a systematic approach to the technology of domestic design, with the possibilities of a wider ranging application.

Several of the concepts arrived at contribute to later designs for a house for his farming property at Eugowra, 230 miles west of Sydney. The farming property allowed him 'to get back to that other scale of architecture, cattleyards and sheds, and the opportunity for making things with your own hands'. Living in the old homestead on the site had revealed both the strengths and weaknesses of the vernacular solution.

The lessons learnt from this building remain recognizable in his own house designs. Throughout all modifications the traditional symmetrical plan and overhanging north verandah persist.

The three distinct phases of the development of the solution, from the Palm Beach house to the final design for the country house, are each in their own way revealing of the experimental nature of the project.

The design for the Palm Beach house shows a large symmetrical dwelling on two levels related to the slope of the north facing site. The corrugated asbestos sheeting that roofs the building curves down and continues as wall cladding on the southern face. The structure combines two distinct building operations, poured concrete and precise prefabricated timber components. The lower level forms a solid concrete podium, on which the lightweight upper level is rested. Both sections could be in production at the same time.

The house was experimental particularly in its relationship to this high-class joinery shop. The project explored the possibilities of housing

Existing farmhouse, Eugowra

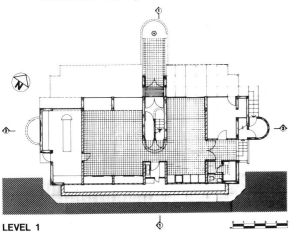

LEVEL 1

Palm Beach house, main living area plan

development based on mass production of timber sections, rather than the usual approach of simply mass organization. It was expected that this would achieve speed of building and a superior quality of construction and finish. With the architect and builder involved from the outset, the building could be designed in direct relationship to the way it was to be constructed. The final drawings evidence a high degree of refinement in both plan and structure. Andrews claims, 'as many drawings were produced for this house as for the whole of the Cameron Offices!'

The initial design for the country house, 1977, adapts this construction concept to rural conditions. The use of two clearly defined building operations appeared particularly relevant in that situation where, because of distances to be travelled, trades needed to be as independent of each other as possible.

At Eugowra the rainfall is low, vegetation sparse, and temperatures can range from 42 degrees C in the summer to zero in the winter. The site for the new house was selected on almost level ground between the existing cottage with its recently-completed barn and bunk sleeping quarters, and a nearby spring channelled to create a small pool, which in turn feeds into a dam. Prevailing breezes pass over this water to the new house site. A solitary tree provides some shade from the western sun.

The available accommodation allowed for a much smaller house with one main bedroom plus guest room. The plan of this single-storey dwelling, despite some relocation of functions, closely resembles that of the upper level of the Palm Beach house.

The physical conditions of site and climate were paramount in determining the solution. The local expertise in underground concrete tank production was to be utilized in the construction of the foundations. The house was designed to quite literally sit over the tanks to hold the sole water supply – that collected from the roof. This would stabilize the floor temperature of the house at a comfortable level in all seasons.

The upper section was designed with a simple bolted mortice and tendon frame, suitable for prepackaging in Sydney. The frame was clad with glass and corrugated galvanized iron sheeting – one of Australia's

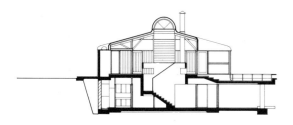

Palm Beach house, section 1

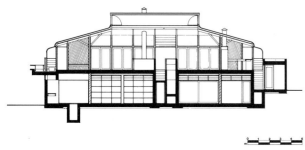

Palm Beach house, section 2

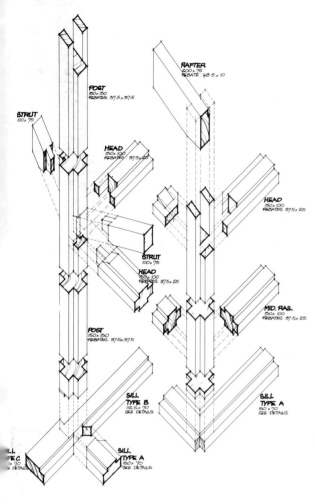

Joinery details, Palm Beach house

cheapest and most adaptable materials. A subtle distinction was made between the role of the roofing iron and that of the walls. For the roof the channels in the corrugation run vertically to facilitate the collection of water, while below the gutters they are laid in the horizontal direction. Sliding glass doors were placed to create breezeways through the house, and large curved roof vents were designed to release the hot air rising from the major spaces, and to allow light directly to the interior. The country style of a verandah on all four sides of the house was modified according to the particular conditions of the exposure, to form uncovered terraces and partially shaded and totally roofed verandahs.

The design remains that of a traditional Australian homestead, held low and close to the earth, and sheltered by its simple, sloping roof.

In the final scheme, 1979, the use of prefabricated timber components was abandoned in favour of the current rural technology of bolted steel sections – 'The language of today's barns and hay sheds that I should have used from the beginning'. The dimensions of the house were rationalized throughout to provide the economy and ease of use of common sized steel members.

Andrews has always had the ability to communicate the essence of his solutions, but rarely has achieved the clarity of expression shown in the stylized design for this small building. With alacrity and wit it sets forth his reply to the climate, resources and customs of the outback.

The basic house with its shading verandahs and pergolas remains unchanged, but the water collection and storage tanks are brought above ground and become strong visual elements as squat cylinders of corrugated iron, boldly placed directly under the overhanging eaves which project from the recessed corners of the main building and adjacent garage.

Light and air flow through the perimeter walls is controlled by the use of modular units of corner doors with double hung balanced ventilation units, sliding glass doors, and fixed tank-iron panels. These panels, together with the 45-degree internal walls, provide the bracing for the frame.

165

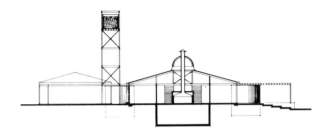

Section, first design house at Eugowra

Under construction

The timber partitions rise to door height only. This allows direct sun rays that enter through the translucent ends of the ridge vault to move through the building. The general internal lighting, both natural and artificial, is indirectly diffused from the white lining of the vault.

From over the fireplace in the heart of the house rises the energy tower. The solar heat collector and tank cap this steel frame skeleton which houses the elevated pressure water tank with its windmill to generate the energy to feed the water up from the storage tanks. Water from the tower is also to be used to spray the iron roof under extreme heat conditions.

The practical solution with its all-encompassing roof, bulging water tanks and erect energy tower becomes highly symbolic of sustenance and shelter under stringent conditions. The power of the imagery comes from the humour and drama inherent in the visual rape of what still remains as an affectionate restatement of the vernacular homestead. The Andrews' country house indicates new directions but at the same time elevates, rather than discounts, common tried and proven rural practices.

The three house designs exhibit an attitude to the distinct physical and cultural characteristics of Australia as respected foundations for contemporary creativity. They show Andrews at his most inventive, and have implications for the future beyond the limited extent of the particular undertaking.

House at Eugowra

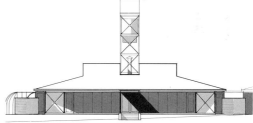

North elevation, house at Eugowra

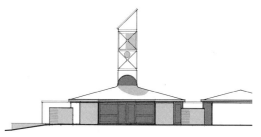

West elevation, house at Eugowra

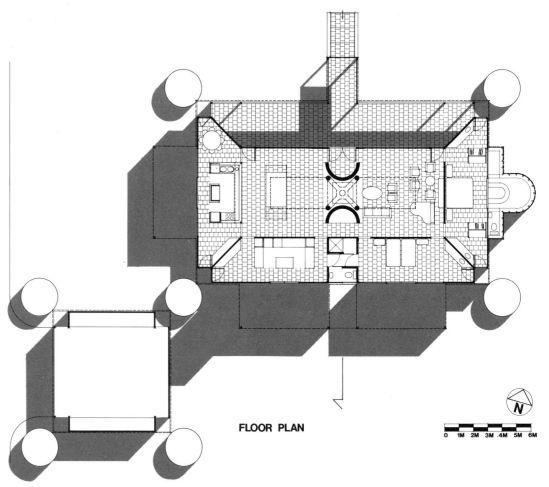

FLOOR PLAN

0 1M 2M 3M .4M 5M 6M

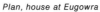

Plan, house at Eugowra

In 1979 as juror for The Australian National Archives Building and Parliament House Competitions, and as an invited entrant for the international Intelsat Headquarters Competition, Andrews became both assessor and assessed. These experiences convinced him that open competitions, whilst ideal in the opportunity they provide, only make sense for buildings of moderate size. Restricted competition being seen as far more satisfactory for major projects that require a large support organization – 'the inexperienced winner simply gets devoured'.

The selection as architect for the Intelsat Headquarters to be built in Washington D.C. has considerable implications for Andrews's future, as for the first time since establishing an office in Sydney he has undertaken work outside Australia.

International outer space

Intelsat is an international company, of 102 member countries, which owns and controls communication satellites. The nature of its charter compelled it to search internationally for an architect. After an initial survey 100 architects from 26 countries were invited to submit proposals; of these six were selected to compete for the final stage.

The proposed building is clearly a summation of the past ten years' work. Evident in its design are the through link path and roof gardens of the Cameron Offices, the development of the theme of office – courtyard modules as found in the original Woden Offices design, the continuation of the utilization of passive energy systems as initially explored in the thwarted Monarto plan, the use of the protective sun shields of King George Tower, and the clean articulation of served and service spaces as in the RMIT Union and Library.

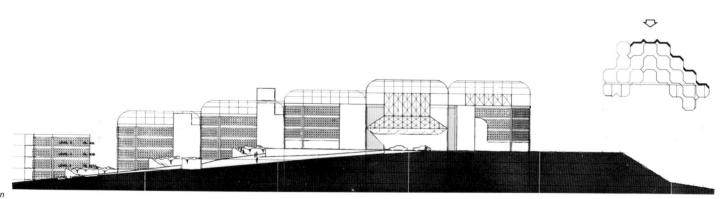

North elevation

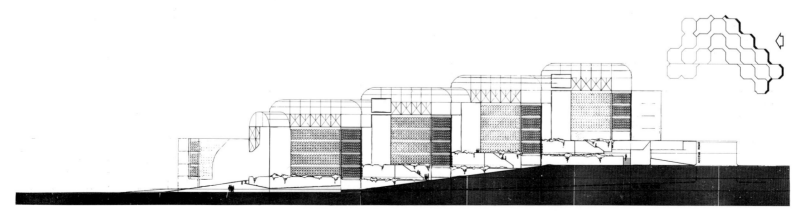

West elevation

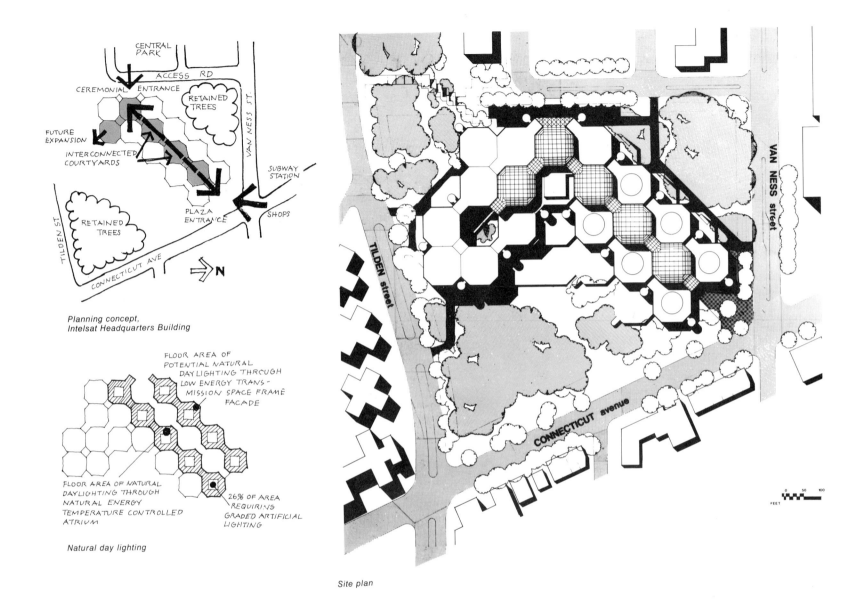

Planning concept,
Intelsat Headquarters Building

FLOOR AREA OF
POTENTIAL NATURAL
DAY LIGHTING THROUGH
LOW ENERGY TRANS-
MISSION SPACE FRAME
FACADE

FLOOR AREA OF NATURAL
DAYLIGHTING THROUGH
NATURAL ENERGY
TEMPERATURE CONTROLLED
ATRIUM

26% OF AREA
REQUIRING
GRADED ARTIFICIAL
LIGHTING

Natural day lighting

Site plan

The site for the Intelsat Headquarters is a 12-acre tree-covered north facing slope in the international precinct approached from a public thoroughfare and a proposed nearby subway station from below, and from a complex of major chancellary buildings from above.

In response to the requirements for growth in three stages, and a window with view from all office desks, Andrews again deployed the eight-sided modules that allow for future additions and afford a high ratio of perimeter office space. Here they step down the slope and accommodate the parking tucked in below and behind the terraces. The units are linked along, and across bridges over, the landscape formed by the row of 86-foot wide courtyards. The complex is entered from each end of this spine, and from the higher ceremonial entrance the full extent of the building is revealed down the central axis of the connected courts.

The most significant aspect of the solution is the balanced integration of techniques to lower energy consumption through the collective efforts of architect, mechanical engineer and landscape architect.

Large clumps of fine old trees were retained on the site for shading and to aid the cooling of the prevailing winds that rise because of the natural chimney effect of the slope. The courtyards are roofed by glazed space frames and are vented to funnel the natural air currents into the interior. The independent stair towers are planned to operate as air ducts to the basement plant rooms. As the courtyards are climatically controlled and shelter their enclosing walls, only half the perimeter walls of the building are subjected to ambient temperature fluctuations. Walls that are exposed to the sun are protected by external filters. The design allows for much use of natural lighting, and excess heat generated within the building is stored in banks until required.

Landscaping on all roof terraces, and planting and ponding in the courtyards and on the roofs of the exterior plant rooms have been provided to contribute to the insulation and cooling of the building.

Andrews has made an expressive and compelling statement out of the factors that conditioned the building's form. The tiered levels, luxurious landscaping, and the faceted translucent panels of the enclosing vertical and overhead space frames, produce an ethereal quality evocative of images of nineteenth-century greenhouses. Yet while the edges of the building are rendered indistinct, even ambiguous, the ordering of the underlying steel structure remains evident.

This is a visually strong work of late twentieth-century architecture with promise as a model for conscious design from a passive energy approach.

ENERGY USAGE
in BTUs per sq. ft per annum

Washington mean	This project
65 000
Utility energy input	24 500
Utility energy input
	29 950
Natural energy input
65 000
Energy usage	54 450
Energy usage
65 000
Utility energy
to be paid for	24 500
Utility energy
to be paid for

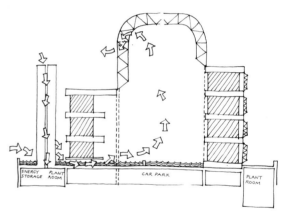

Section showing induced air movement

And on to . . .

In the 1967 Boyer lectures for the Australian Broadcasting Commission the architect-critic, Robin Boyd, strongly condemned the dependency of Australian architecture on borrowed ideas, and the lack of original progressive thought from within the country. He regretted the absence of Andrews who he claimed was 'characteristically Australian by birth, training, attitude, speech, manner and by his inability to find a satisfying outlet for original talent here at home'. That changed with the Cameron Offices, yet ironically the opportunity to bring to realization many of the concepts he has been pursuing during his time in Australia came from an international client for a building in America.

When Andrews returned to Sydney he said he would stay as long as his work remained productive. Isolation from the mainstream of contact and comment has had little effect on his ways, so today it cannot be said that the Australian profession is lacking a vital and challenging local stimulus. Andrews is building an architecture with far reaching meaning and relevance – this gives it, and him, an unique place in the history of architecture of the country. The award of the Royal Australian Institute of Architects, 1980 Gold Medal and the honour of Officer of the Order of Australia, 1981, acknowledged his contributions to the advancement of architecture.

The opportunity to embark on exploratory routes does not come easily. Much of Andrews' success has come from his ability to convince the client of the value of what are sometimes radical departures from the conventional solutions. Innovative programs of any sort contain risks. But without the perception of the architect and the support of the client, architecture cannot hope to respond to the changing demands placed upon it. Andrews belongs amongst a world-wide small group of architects with the ability to think fundamental issues afresh and the talent to explore the way in search of better places for living. His strength here lies in the depth of his convictions and his courage to act upon them.

Jennifer Taylor

Model, Intelsat Headquarters Building

Projects, publications, film

Projects

Dates refer to the commencement of planning and design
1962
Scarborough College Master Plan
Scarborough, Ontario, Canada
Development plan/preliminary design for a new satellite college of the University of Toronto providing facilities for education in the sciences and humanities.

1963
Scarborough College Phase I
Military Road, Scarborough, Ontario, Canada
The nucleus of a new university extending along a ridgetop around an internal pedestrian street.

1964
Erindale College Master Plan
Erindale, Ontario, Canada
Development plan for a new satellite college of the University of Toronto.

1965
Bellmere Public School
Scarborough, Ontario, Canada
A single storey school for Kindergarten to Grade 6 students located in a suburban residential district. Individual classrooms are expressed and grouped informally in four wings around a central assembly hall. Expansion was anticipated at the classroom wings.

1965
Student Housing Complex B
University of Guelph, Ontario, Canada
A student residence and dining facilities for 1760 students. Over 60 per cent of the students live in single rooms and many of the doubles have separate study rooms. The form and organization of the project is the direct result of a sociological study of student behavioural patterns.

1965
Apartment Tower for the Stelco Steel Company
Experimental study demonstrating possible new uses of steel. The scheme applies automotive technology to problems of housing and postulates a tower structure that would serve as a 'filing cabinet' for prefabricated steel dwelling units.

1965
African Place, Expo '67
Montreal, Quebec, Canada
A multi-use area of temporary nature permitting demounting if desired. It was required to provide a series of exhibition environments for various African nations whose space requirements were not known.

1965
Activity Area F, Expo '67
Montreal, Quebec, Canada
One of a series of commercial groupings designed to provide linkage between major exhibition areas and space for a variety of concessions.

1965
Commonwealth Place, Expo '67
Montreal, Quebec, Canada
(Not built)
A cluster of fibreglass units providing Commonwealth countries with independent exhibition spaces.

1966
Master Plan Framework Report
St George Campus, University of Toronto
Ontario, Canada
Document 1 – Master Plan
Document 2 – The Conduit System
Plan for future growth of the downtown campus west of St George Street.

1967
Prince of Wales College
Charlottetown, Prince Edward Island
Canada
Planning study and implementation of first phase development including a lecture theatre, a boiler plant and alterations to the existing building.

1967
Weldon Library, University of Western Ontario
London, Ontario, Canada
A library with a capacity of one million volumes and study facilities for 2000 students.

1967
Metro Centre
Toronto, Ontario, Canada
A development plan and program for 200 acres of railway land strategic to the redevelopment of downtown Toronto. It incorporates the city's major transportation exchange, approximately 7 000 000 square feet of integrated office and retail space, 9000 residential units, a hotel complex, a communication tower and television studios.
Stage 1, the C.N. Tower (as redesigned in 1970) completed construction in 1977.

1967
Student Centre, University of Toronto
Toronto, Canada
(Not built)
A non-academic support facility for faculty and students including a theatre and dining recreational and commercial facilities.

1967
Miami Seaport Passenger Terminal
Miami, Florida, USA
A passenger ship terminal based on an extensive analysis of traffic patterns and providing facilities and services for international trade and cruise travel.

1967
City of Hamilton Civic Square Study
Hamilton, Toronto, Canada
A competition entry for the comprehensive redevelopment of the business administration area of downtown Hamilton providing for public and commercial use and their inter-relationship, with options for future development. Placed second.

1967
Yorkdale Shopping Centre
Toronto, Ontario, Canada
Development plan and implementation studies for the future growth of a metropolitan sub-centre.

1967
Student Residence, Brock University
St Catherines, Ontario, Canada
A residence for 380 students with dining and recreational facilities. The design is based on the concept of apartment type units consisting of two double rooms and two single rooms sharing a lounge, kitchen and washroom.

1967
Sarah Lawrence College Library Instructional Centre
Bronxville, New York, USA
(Not built)
A three-floor integrated complex of flexible teaching and library spaces relating to surrounding buildings and incorporating pedestrian movement at the mid level and facilities requiring heavy service access at ground level.

1968
Gund Hall, Harvard Graduate School of Design
Harvard University, Cambridge, Massachusetts, USA
Studios of each department are gathered into one open integrated environment by a sloping trussed roof over five overlapping floors each containing one department. A pedestrian colonnade and internal street giving access to common facilities are provided at street level.

1968
Cameron Offices
Belconnen, ACT, Australia
General office space and communal facilities for 4000 Government employees arranged around a public pedestrian mall in seven wings separated by landscaped courtyards. The complex established the first phase of the town centre of a satellite town of Canberra.

1968
Smith College Art Complex
Northampton, Massachusetts, USA
Skylit fine arts studios, an art gallery and library are organized around an internal pedestrian street and covered courtyard.

1969
David Mirvish Gallery
Toronto, Ontario, Canada
A well known Toronto Victorian residential streetscape is maintained by the retention and conversion of an existing house together with a discreet rear addition to provide a variety of exhibition spaces for the new gallery.

1969
Scarborough College, Phase II
Scarborough, Ontario, Canada
Instead of expanding the first stage of Scarborough College longitudinally, it was found that better use of Phase I facilities would occur if future expansion radiated from the existing hub facilities. The Phase II building provides flexible office and laboratory space, together with an indoor sporting complex.

1970
School of Art, Kent State
Kent State University, Kent via Cleveland, Ohio, USA
This building provides flexible and spatially varied studio space, utilizing a steel frame with translucent insulated fibreglass wall panels and skylights. Its organization optimizes interaction amongst students.

1970
Canadian National Tower, Metro Centre
Toronto, Ontario, Canada
The CN Tower, Stage 1 of Metro Centre, is the world's tallest freestanding structure being 1815 feet, 15 inches in height. The tower

incorporates transmitters for television and radio as well as observation decks and revolving restaurant above a tapering, three pronged, post-tensioned, reinforced concrete shaft.

1970
Feasibility Study for Expansion of the Behavioural Sciences Department
Tufts University, Medford, Massachusetts, USA
A terraced infill development, preserving the visual character of existing hilltop buildings as viewed from below. At the same time, the views from the established courtyard between existing hilltop buildings are maintained.

1970
King George Tower
Corner King and George Streets, Sydney, Australia
A triangulated multi-storey building on Australia's busiest pedestrian intersection providing continuous shops and covered sidewalks at pedestrian level together with a sunny plaza. These areas are designed to be connected to adjoining and opposite buildings below street level.

1970
Student Residence, Australian National University
Canberra, ACT, Australia
Six student rooms grouped around common facilities are stacked to produce a four-floor building that wanders along a creek bank and incorporates a pedestrian street at ground level.

1972
Pintannie Commercial Redevelopment
Roma Street, Brisbane, Queensland, Australia
(Not built)
A multi-storey office complex on a large site close to the Brisbane City Hall, incorporating retail facilities and public open spaces at pedestrian levels.

1972
Belconnen Town Centre Retail Mall Study
Belconnen, Canberra, ACT, Australia
A framework design for the retail, parking and office facilities of the Belconnen Town Centre around a vaulted mall extending from Cameron Offices to Lake Gininderra.

1973
Woden East Government Offices
Woden, Canberra, ACT, Australia
(Not built)
Interconnecting walk up office modules suspended above a flood plain. A mid level independent public walkway gives direct access to each module and connects to the adjacent town centre pedestrian system.

1973
Student Residence, Canberra College of Advanced Education
Canberra, ACT, Australia
Six student rooms each with northern views are arranged around common facilities with direct access to open street stairs. Each such group is terraced above a similar group between a pair of street stairs.

1973
Chemical Engineering Building, University of Queensland
St Lucia, Brisbane, Queensland, Australia
Staff offices, teaching areas and specialist laboratory areas wrap around a sky and side-lit three storey high laboratories filled with tall experimental equipment of various heights. A public walkway to residential colleges beyond is also incorporated.

1973
Design Guidelines for the Retention of the Great Hall, Metro Centre
Toronto, Ontario, Canada
Urban design guidelines for the retention of the Great Hall of Union Station in the Metro Centre redevelopment within a reorganized network of transportation facilities, pedestrian routes and public open spaces.

1973
Kelvin Grove College of Advanced Education Master Plan
Kelvin Grove, Brisbane, Queensland, Australia
Plan for the future development of an existing college on a hilltop of Brisbane.

1974
Darling Downs Institute of Advanced Education Development Plan Study
Toowoomba, Queensland, Australia
Plan for the future development of a newly established tertiary education institution on a flat, windswept semi-rural site around an interconnecting pedestrian street.

1974
Ithaca Technical College Development Plan Study
Brisbane, Queensland, Australia
Development of educational facilities on a site bisected by a creek and a proposed new arterial road.

1974
Regional Shopping Centre
Sydney, NSW, Australia
(Not built)
Two three-floor department stores are located adjacent to each other separated only by specialty shops and a vaulted common access concourse as they step down a hillside. Direct service access is provided on the lower two levels and parking structures on both sides give direct shopper access to all levels. Professional offices are located in terrace fashion on the face of each shopping level as it steps down the hill.

1974
Belconnen Town Centre Study
Belconnen, Canberra, ACT, Australia
Design study of the major retail centre of Belconnen to be located north of Cameron Offices by the Belconnen Town Centre Trust, brief requirements being considerably increased since the 1972 study.

1974
Transportation Interchange and Commercial/Sporting Development Study
Canberra, ACT, Australia
Preliminary design of the major bus terminal and rapid transit station in central Canberra, linked to integrated indoor sporting facilities and residential accommodation.

1975
School of Australian Environmental Studies
Griffith University, Brisbane, Queensland, Australia
A courtyard building housing laboratories, classrooms and staff offices stepping down a tree covered slope from the ridge top pedestrian spine of the University.

1975
Little Bay Low Income Housing Scheme
Little Bay, Sydney, Australia
Subsidized rental housing for 46 families, 32 aged persons and 29 childless couples terraced and clustered around eight private streets at a site density of 153 persons per hectare.

1975
Environmental Guidelines Study
Palm Beach, NSW, Australia
Guidelines for the protection and reinforcement of the unique environmental quality of this scenic seaside suburb of Sydney.

1975
Monarto Town Centre Urban Design Study
Monarto, South Australia, Australia
Design of town centre facilities to utilize low energy principles. The Centre extends from a hilltop transportation terminal and water tower to a man-made lake around a sequence of public squares cooled by ponds falling from the tower to the lake. Proposed buildings also utilized solar energy.

1975
Ipswich College of Technical and Further Education Master Plan Study
Ipswich, Queensland, Australia
This plan for the development of a new educational institution provides a spinal organization of facilities around a hilltop linked to a railway station on the Brisbane suburban network.

1976
Andrews Houses
Palm Beach, NSW, Australia
(Not built)
A new house for John Andrews and his changing family requirements utilizing the traditional Australian house form with adaptations to a seaside/rain forest setting and currently available building materials and methods. A smaller version was designed close by for his mother.

1976
Educational Resource Centre
Kelvin Grove College of Advanced Education
Brisbane, Queensland, Australia
This major central facility of the college interconnects three existing buildings around the Main Court of the College to provide an appropriate hilltop focus to departmental facilities located on the slopes of the hill.

1976
Darling Downs Institute of Advanced Education Development Plan Study
Toowoomba, Queensland, Australia
Further development and reassessment of the 1974 plan in view of severe Government cutbacks in educational spending.

1976
Belconnen Bus Terminal
Belconnen, ACT, Australia
First stage of a transportation interchange located between Cameron Offices and the relocated retail centre of Belconnen. A rapid transit station will be incorporated at a later stage.

1977
Library/Union Stage 1
Royal Melbourne Institute of Technology
Melbourne, Victoria, Australia
The core campus facilities are organized with Union facilities located around existing student movement areas at ground levels and the library as an upper level infill between three surrounding buildings. The development incorporates a major entrance to the downtown campus from Swanston Street.

1977
Museum of Australia Site Location Study
Canberra, ACT, Australia
Development of the concept and brief for Australia's national museum put forward by the Piggot Committee in 1975 and the assessment of alternative sites in terms of this concept and requirements.

1977
Sydney Central Station Development Study
Sydney, NSW, Australia
A proposal to provide better facilities for passengers using this major transportation centre of Sydney, particularly with regard to connections between buses, suburban trains and interstate and country trains. The proposal provides for extensive restoration and renovation of the existing landmark buildings, and the addition of new facilities in the most sympathetic manner.

1977
Woden College of Technical and Further Education
Woden, Canberra, ACT, Australia
After the abandonment of plans for the Woden East Government Offices at tender stage in 1975 due to Government policy changes, the NCDC decided that the project would suitably accommodate the requirements of a proposed College of Technical and Further Education. Three modules are being constructed in Stage 1.

1977
Lecture Theatre and Staff Office Buildings
Darling Downs Institute of Advanced Education
Toowoomba, Queensland, Australia
Primarily a teaching building used by all departments of the Institute. It is designed as an important central link in the pedestrian spine of the Institute incorporating courtyards to provide shelter from prevailing winds.

1977
Mandurah High School
Mandurah, Western Australia
(Not built)
A prototype which allows easy adaption to change as curricula develops and organization changes, this building

incorporates natural lighting, ventilation, heating and cooling by way of skylights, a bore water roof reticulation system and the provision of courtyards in its modular building system.

1978
Resource Material Centre, Ipswich College of Technical and Further Education,
Ipswich, Queensland, Australia
Core facilities for the new campus resulting from the 1975 Master Plan Study. Union and Arts and Crafts facilities are located at pedestrian levels with library facilities above.

1978
Proposal for a Housing Village, Griffith University
Brisbane, Queensland, Australia
Preliminary design of a housing village accommodating staff, students and nurses of a nearby hospital in self contained clusters and collegiate type units organised along the contours of a magnificent sloping bushland site. The complex was designed to provide all accommodation requirements for visiting athletes to the 1982 Commonwealth Games, with minor adaptation of Stage I provisions which could later be converted for use as a University service facilities.

1978
Andrews's Farmhouse
Eugowra, NSW, Australia
Further development of the idea of Palm Beach, utilizing the traditional Australian house form incorporating solar and wind energy concepts and responding to the construction constraints of an isolated country site.

1978
Bateman Catholic Centre
Perth, Western Australia
Further development of the Mandurah High School ideas to incorporate a preschool, primary school, church and presbytery as well as a secondary school.

1978
Union and Other Facilities Building, Royal Melbourne Institute of Technology
Melbourne, Victoria, Australia
Cutbacks in Government spending leading to a change in brief and master planning requirements, the first stage of this project now accommodates student union facilities. Like the 1977 project, these are located around existing student movement areas at ground levels. Stage II will expand these facilities and provide a new 4 level library at upper levels. The project is designed to accommodate a further 5 floors of academic space, linking and infilling between existing buildings and possible adjoining redevelopment.

1979
Cluster Housing Project
Glebe, Sydney, NSW, Australia
(pending)
This project provides clusters of duplex 1 and 2 bedroom units organised around elevated pedestrian precincts, achieving a density of 330 persons per hectare within a 3 floor height limitation.

1980
Intelsat Headquarters Building, Washington, DC, USA
Winner of an invited international design competition, this three stage project will provide convention, office and technical facilities for the operation and control of satellites operated by the International Telecommunications Satellite Organization. The project utilizes low energy principles, being organized around a network of covered atriums stepping down a magnificent tree-covered slope.

1980
Garden Island Parking Structure
Woolloomooloo Bay, Sydney, NSW, Australia
This structure channels Cowper Wharf Roadway around it to provide easy access to its 1250 parking spaces. The structure defines a new edge to Woolloomooloo Bay, together with new naval wharfs. Its location preserves and reinstates a lost but historic cliff face and provides a new park at the base of the cliff for residents of Woolloomooloo. Its rooftop provides landscaped areas with commanding views and tennis courts for the residents of Potts Point and workers of the adjoining Garden Island Naval Depot.

1980
Woolloomooloo Housing Scheme
Woolloomooloo, Sydney, NSW, Australia
This medium density housing scheme at the periphery of historic Woolloomooloo, provides 15 stacked 1, 2 and 3 bedroom units in 4–5 floor building forms maintaining the scale and character of the area at approximately 3 times greater density than terrace houses of the Woolloomooloo basin.

Publications
'Toronto City Hall and Square Competition'
The Architect and Building News
vol. 214, 15 October 1958, pp 509–517
(Toronto City Hall and Square Competition)

'Toronto City Hall and Square Competition'
Royal Architecture Institute of Canada Journal
vol. 35, October 1958, pp 372–3
(Toronto City Hall and Square Competition)

'University Studies'
Royal Architecture Institute of Canada Journal
vol. 41, No. 7, July 1964, pp 61–6
(Scarborough College)

'Feature'
Royal Architecture Institute of Canada Journal
vol. 41, No. 7, July 1964, p 15
(Bellmere Public School)

'Panel Discussion of the Toronto City Hall and Square Competition'
Royal Architecture Institute of Canada Journal
vol. 42, No. 9, September 1965, pp 38–55
(Toronto City Hall and Square Competition)

'U.B.C. Competition'
Royal Architecture Institute of Canada Journal
vol. 42, No. 9, September 1965, pp 64–5
(Student Union Competition – University of British Columbia)

'New Campus Rises in Canada'
Architectural Record
vol. 138, No. 5, November 1965, p 62
(Scarborough College)

Newman, Oscar. 'The New Campus: It suggests a changed scale in urban architecture'
Architectural Forum
vol. 124, No. 4, May 1966, pp 30–55
(Scarborough College)

'Scarborough College, Ontario'
The Canadian Architect
vol. 11, No. 5, May 1966, pp 41–62
(Scarborough College)

'Expo '67'
Royal Architecture Institute of Canada Journal
vol. 43, No. 7, July 1966, p 46
(African Place)

Donat, John (ed.) *World Architecture 3*
London 1966
Publisher: Studio Vista
pp 171–7
(Scarborough College)

'Bellmere Public School, Scarborough, Ontario'
The Canadian Architect
vol. 11, No. 8, August 1966, pp 54–6
(Bellmere Public School)

'Beyond the Individual Building'
Architectural Record
vol. 140, No. 3, September 1966, pp 161–72
(Scarborough College 161–4; Bellmere Public School 165; African Place 166; Apartment Building Project 167; Student Residence – Guelph University 168–9; Master Plan University of Toronto 170–1; Red Coach Inn 172)

'Closed Circuit'
Architectural Review
vol. 140, No. 836, October 1966, pp 245–52
(Scarborough College)

'College Scarborough Universite de Toronto Ontario'
l'architecture aujourdhui
vol. 37, No. 129, Decembre 1966/Janvier 1967, pp 84–90
(Scarborough College)

'Scarborough College, Ontario'
The Canadian Architect Year Book
1966, pp 64–6
(Scarborough College)

'Guelph'
Architecture Canada
vol. 44, No. 1, January 1967, p 27
(Student Residence, University of Guelph)

'''Colleges'' A Satellite Built for T.V.'
Time
vol. 89, No. 2, 13 January 1967, pp 46–8
(Scarborough College)

'Student Residences, University of Guelph, Ontario'
The Canadian Architect
vol. 12, No. 2, February 1967, pp 57–62
(Student Residences, University of Guelph)

Frampton, Kenneth. 'Scarborough College, Ontario, Canada'
Architectural Design
vol. 37, No. 4, April 1967, pp 178–87
(Scarborough College)

Brown, Harry Faulkner. 'Canada 1967'
Royal Institute of British Architects Journal
vol. 74, No. 4, April 1967, pp 143–57
(Scarborough College)

'Bellmere and Guelph'
Architectural Review
vol. 141, No. 843, May 1967, pp 324–5
(Bellmere Public School, Student Residence Guelph University)

'Scarborough'
Architecture Canada
vol. 44, No. 6, June 1967, p 52
(Scarborough College)

'Expo '67 Montreal'
Baumeister
vol. 64, Juni 1967, whole issue
(African Place)

Russel, P. 'J. Andrews Scarborough College'
Arts Canada
vol. 24 (insert), August/September 1967
(Scarborough College)

'Canadian Architecture Abroad'
Architecture Canada
vol. 44, No. 9, September 1967, p 40
(Miami Passenger Terminal)

'Portfolio: Architecture'
Perspecta 11 The Yale Architectural Journal
1967, pp 178–215
(Apartment Building Project 182; Scarborough College 214–15)

'Housing Complex "B", Phase I, University of Guelph, Ontario, Canada'
Progressive Architecture
vol. 49, No. 7, July 1968, p 126
(Student Residences, University of Guelph)

'Scarborough College, Phase II, University of Toronto, Canada'
Progressive Architecture
vol. 49, No. 7, July 1968, pp 114–15
(Scarborough College Phase II)

Smith, Kenneth B., 'Dorm City'
Architectural Forum
vol. 129, No. 5, December 1968, pp 76–85
(Student Residences – University of Guelph)

'Toronto Confronts the Lake'
Architectural Forum
vol. 130, No. 1, January 1969, pp 112–13
(Metro Centre)

'Building Projects for Downtown Toronto'
Architecture Canada
vol. 46, No. 2, February 1969, pp 29–36
(Metro Centre 32–3)

'City Within a City'
The Architect and Building News
vol. 3, No. 3, 5 June 1969, pp 30–4
(Proposed Metro Centre Redevelopment)

'Harvard Graduate School of Design; the new building, just begun, promises communications among all

Departments'
Architectural Forum
vol. 131, No. 5, December 1969, pp 62–4
(Gund Hall)

Prangnell, Peter. 'Some Comments on the Building'
Architectural Forum
vol. 131, No. 5, December 1969, pp 65–7
(Gund Hall)

'$1 Billion Dollar Program to Catch the Imagination'
Habitat (Canada)
vol. 12, No. 1, December 1969, pp 17–19
(Metro Centre)

'Harvard Graduate School of Design'
Architectural and Engineering News
January 1970, pp 20–1
(Gund Hall)

'Design and Process: four projects by the John Andrews office'
Architectural Record
vol. 147, No. 2, February 1970, pp 131–46
(Belconnen Government Office Complex 132–5; Metro Centre 136–9; Gund Hall 140–2; Library Instruction Centre Sarah Lawrence College 143–5)

'Half Mile Gangplank'
Architectural Forum
vol. 132, No. 2, March 1970, pp 54–7
(Miami Passenger Terminal)

'Passenger Terminal, Port of Miami'
The Canadian Architect
vol. 15, No. 4, April 1970, pp 42–51
(Miami Passenger Terminal)

'The Focus is People'
Japan Architect
vol. 45, No. 7, July 1970, pp 44–5
(John Andrews)

'Student Residences, Brock University'
The Canadian Architect
vol. 15, No. 11, November 1970, pp 31–5
(Student Residences, Brock University)

'Annual Awards'
The Canadian Architect Year Book
1970, pp 27–54
(Metro Centre; Belconnen Government Office Complex)

'Belconnen Offices'
Constructional Review
vol. 44, No. 2, May 1971, pp 46–52
(Belconnen Government Office Complex)

Ede, Carol Moore. *Canadian Architecture 1960–70*
Toronto, 1971
Publisher: Burns & MacEachern
pp 24–35
(Scarborough College)

'Annual Awards'
The Canadian Architect
vol. 16, No. 2, December 1971, pp 33–60
(Behavioural Sciences Building, Tufts University)

'Student Residences, Guelph'
Design and Environment
vol. 1, No. 1, Winter 1971, pp 32–3
(Student Residences, University of Guelph)

'Conversations with the John Andrews Architects'
Progressive Architecture
vol. 54, February 1972, pp 62–75

(Gund Hall 63; McMaster Student Centre, McMaster University 64; Georgian Lake Cottage 64; Behavioural Sciences Building Tufts University 65; School of Art, Kent State University 66–7; Art Complex, Smith College 68; Scarborough College Phase II 69; Hooker Tower 70–71; Belconnen Government Office Complex 73; St Paul Campus Plan, University of Minnesota 74; Metro Centre 75).

'Designing for Growth: The Metamorphosis of a Rural Campus into a University Town'
Architectural Record
vol. 151, No. 5, May 1972, pp 89–98
(Student Residences, University of Guelph 95–6)

Ackland, J. H. 'Voice: Metro Centre: the case of premature architecture'
Canadian Architect
vol. 17, May 1972, pp 50, 62
(Metro Centre)

'Glass Horizons'
Architectural Forum
vol. 136, No. 5, June 1972, p 7
(Gund Hall)

'Gund Hall: Harvard's Graduate School of Design under one roof'
Architectural Record
vol. 152, No. 6, November 1972, pp 95–104
(Gund Hall)

'D. B. Weldon Library, University of Western Ontario, London'
The Canadian Architect
vol. 17, November 1972, pp 26–69
(Weldon Library)

'D. B. Weldon Library'
Architectural Forum
vol. 132, No. 11, November 1972, p 6
(Weldon Library)

Marlin, W. 'Harvard's New Hall'
Architectural Forum
vol. 137, No. 5, December 1972, pp 50–5
(Gund Hall)

Drew, Phillip. *Third Generation: The Changing Meaning of Architecture*
London 1972, pp 144–51
Publisher: Pall Mall Press
(African Place 145; Scarborough College 146–7; Student Residences University of Guelph 148; Miami Passenger Terminal 149; Belconnen Government Office Complex 149; Gund Hall 150; Metro Centre 151)

Huxtable, Ada Louise. 'Good architecture – bad vibes'
Canadian Architect (Reprinted from the *New York Times*)
vol. 18, No. 1, January 1973, pp 36–45
(George Gund Hall, Harvard University Graduate School of Design)

Du Bois, Macy. 'A Protestant work of Architecture'
Canadian Architect
vol. 18, No. 1, January 1973, pp 40, 42
(George Gund Hall, Harvard University Graduate School of Design)

'Gund Hall'
Architectural Design
vol. 43, No. 2, February 1973, p 117
(Gund Hall)

CN/CP Metro Centre'
Architecture Canada Newsmagazine
vol. 50, February, 1973, p 1
(Metro Centre Tower)

'AIA Awards Programs: George Gund Hall, Harvard Graduate School'
American Institute of Architects Journal
vol. 59, No. 5, May 1973, pp 30–1
(Gund Hall)

'Toronto's Tower'
Architecture Plus
June 1973, pp 9–10
(Metro Centre, Toronto Television Tower)

'John Andrews'
Architecture and Urbanism
No. 41, 74:05, May 1974, pp 25–134
(6 articles, 3 in English, 21 works illustrated)

Chetham, Charles. 'The New Smith College Museum of Art'
The Art Journal
vol. 33, No. 3, Spring 1974, pp 231–7
(Smith College Art Complex)

Haimerl, Duncan. 'Tall . . . Taller . . . Tallest'
Habitat (Canada)
vol. 17, No. 3, 1974, pp 22–5
(The CN Tower)

'Cameron Offices'
Constructional Review
vol. 48, No. 2, May 1975, pp 18–23
(Cameron Offices)

Witzig, John. 'A. A. Interview: John Andrews by John Witzig'
Architecture in Australia
vol. 64, No. 3, June 1975, pp 58–67
(John Andrews)

'Notes from Down Under'
The Canadian Architect
vol. 21, No. 6, June 1976, pp 38–40
(An informal discussion with John Andrews)

'Five Projects by John Andrews International'
The Canadian Architect
vol. 23, No. 7, July 1976, pp 19–39
(Cameron Offices, Canberra 21–5; Woolloomooloo Housing Study, Sydney 26–8; King George Tower, Sydney 29–33; Student Residence, Canberra College 34–6; Woden East Government Offices, Canberra 37–9)

Saunders, David. 'Homes for the Bureaucrats'
Architecture Australia
vol. 65, No. 3, June–July 1976, p 62
(Cameron Offices)

'King George Tower, Sydney'
Constructional Review
vol. 49, No. 3, August 1976, pp 11–19
(King George Tower)

'Getting Chemical Engineers Together'
Architecture Australia
vol. 65, No. 6, January 1977
(Chemical Engineering Building, University of Queensland)

'King George Tower, King & George Streets, Sydney'
NSW Builder
vol. 6, No. 1, February 1977, pp 4–15
(King George Tower)

'Chemical Engineering'
Constructional Review
vol. 50, No. 1, February 1977, pp 28–33
(Chemical Engineering Building, University of Queensland)

Taylor, Jennifer. 'Civil Service City (The Cameron Offices)'
Architectural Review
vol. 163, No. 973, March 1978, pp 136–46
(Cameron Offices)

'The School of Australian Environmental Studies at Griffith University'
The Queensland Master Builder
vol. 15, No. 10, April 1978, pp 13–19
(School of Australian Environmental Studies, Griffith University)

'S.A.E.S.'
Constructional Review
vol. 51, No. 3, August 1978, pp 56–62
(School of Australian Environmental Studies, Griffith University)

'King George Tower, Sydney'
Architectural Review
vol. 164, No. 979, September 1978, pp 140–1
(King George Tower)

'Griffith University, Brisbane'
Architectural Review
vol. 164, No. 979, September 1978, pp 188–9
(School of Australian Environmental Studies, Griffith University)

'Australia's John Andrews wins $30 million competition'
Architectural Record
June 1980, p 37
(Intelsat)

McGregor, Craig. *The Australian People*
Australia 1980, pp 132–9
Publisher: Hodden & Stoughton
'Profile: John Andrews'

Film
'Architecture a Performing Art'
16 mm and 35 mm
Director: Michael Robertson
Film Australia
Eton Road, Lindfield, 2070, NSW, Australia